Fishing Came First

Books by JOHN N. COLE

In Maine
From the Ground Up *(with Charles Wing)*
Striper
Amaranth
Cityside/Countryside *(with Nathan Cobb)*
The Sun Book
Salmon
Breaking New Ground *(with Charles Wing)*
Fishing Came First

Fishing Came First

———

JOHN N. COLE

Lyons & Burford, *Publishers*

Printed in the United States of America
10 9 8 7 6 5 4 3 2

Cole, John N., 1923–
    Fishing came first.
    1. Fishing. I Title.
SH441.C5915   1989   799.1   89-2569
ISBN 1-55821-041-5

FOR JEAN, *who gave me the idea . . .*
AND FOR JEFFREY, *who gave me the fishing*

Key West

February 26, 1988

"I love barracuda," Jeffrey shouts into the careening wind.

Two shadows, two prone posts, rest dark in the center of a white circle of grassless marl sixty feet from the boat drifting toward them. Jeffrey stands on the flat-topped bow, line piled at his feet, right arm raised, holding the fly rod John Graves made for him.

Rude, pushing from the northeast, wind furrows the flat's shoal surfaces. In channels where there is depth enough for gusts to grab, they yank an aquamarine sea into tufted whitecaps and shove them against an ebbing tide, upsetting ordered rhythms.

Pitched higher than the wind's oboe, the flyline's sharp notes are a fife whistling in time with Jeffrey's right arm as he whips his rod back and forth. With each cycle, the line lengthens, pulled by its weight and the strength of Jeffrey's wrist and forearm from the deck. He concentrates on keeping the cast low, where the wind will not pester it as it torments the whitecaps and slaps at our hatbrims, trying to

1

snatch our hats from our heads as it has tried to steal this
fishing day and break our hearts.

I have been in Key West a week, working in a second-
floor office of a former U.S. Navy building on the island's
westernmost shore. From the hall windows at the top of the
stairs, the view spills west from the rim of Key West Harbor, across the buoyed channel, past Tank Island, across the
Lakes Passage, and from there along the string of hummocks dark against the horizon: mangrove and marl knees
rising from under the Gulf's aquamarine coverlet. Mule
Key, Archer Key, Crawfish Key, Barracouta Key, Big
Mullet Key, Cottrell Key, Man Key, Woman Key, and finally Boca Grande Key, the last of the smudges on the horizon I can see from the window.

But the eye of my mind sees farther. Beyond Boca
Grande, across the depths of the Boca Grande Channel, on
the other side of that turbulent first embrace of the Atlantic
and the Gulf, there is the ring of the Marquesas. My inner
vision spans the twenty-five miles from the rim of Key West
Harbor to that slim circle of mangroves, hummocks, and
white sand strips drawn around a shoal lagoon deep in mystery.

Jeffrey and I have been there together, and we shall go
again. If the wind were better behaved, we could have gone
today, but Jeffrey is a prudent captain and knows it would
be foolhardy to test the Boca Grande Channel in his new,
eighteen-foot Maverick, a broad leaf of a boat designed to
float lightly on the thin waters of the flats—that vast, pale
scroll of coral and turtle grass that unrolls from Key West to
the Marquesas and from there to the Tortugas: a shimmering document of secrets scored by channels as elusive as patterns on a butterfly's wing.

In six years of study, Jeffrey has learned to read most of
the scrolls. Like a scholar returning each morning to the

2

same enigmatic manuscript, he guides his skiff at speed over passages he has read many times.

Today's reading has been brief. Restrained by the wind's stinging decree, Jeffrey has brought us to a flat east of Mangrove Key. On this single page of a scroll he has yet to decipher fully, Jeffrey has discovered an assembly of barracuda, gathered here in contradiction of their customary solitude, brought together on a single broad stripe of white and golden sand. Suspended between the transparent surface and the shimmering bottom, the long fish hover in the optimal spot for absorbing heat from February's tentative sun.

Since November, the sea has cooled and, like thin-blooded, pale old men stretched in a seawall's lee with closed eyes turned skyward under lizard, trembling lids, the barracuda fixate on gathering the warmth that pours from above and reflects from below.

But these creatures are neither senile nor asleep.

Their motionless suspension is yet another demonstration of natural adaption: minimal energy expended for maximum energy absorbed. The engines that power these silver fish are never shut down; their receptors that decipher the sea's quick codes are perpetually set at maximum alert. These are fish of prey, undersea raptors who take liquid wing, sight, and stoop with rocketing dives aloft, scattering schools of needlefish like bright rain rising from the sea.

Elongated, pale silver cigars of fish, their three feet of shimmering scales catch the sky in mirrors and toss the sun back at a beholder so cleverly that were it not for its shadow the motionless barracuda of the flats would be invisible, lost in light, gone before it is known to exist. This is how it hunts, waiting, still as glass, the springs of its senses so tightly wound, set for instant release the split second any morsel moves within its ken. Then its broad tail throbs, a rocket ascends pursued by the sword of its shadow, and the barracuda's great elongated jaws are propelled across the sands. Guided by the crisp images decoded in its large, dark eyes, this falcon of the flats rends its quarry with talons of canine teeth so keen that only a gentle flurry of disturbed surface marks the violent passage.

This is the barracuda on its mission. There is also the barracuda at play, and although Jeffrey loves all fish, he proclaims aloud his love for the barracuda because this is a creature of vivacious curiosity, a fish who turns up more often than any other on the flats' pale pages, the only member of the thin-water community who will wander over to investigate a lure or reconnoiter a hull from beneath simply to verify its presence, to place it in the day's catalog.

This curiosity and its inclination to seek the winter sun when most other fish are scattered by the chill mean that if Jeffrey knows where to look, he can almost count on meeting a barracuda in February, no matter how rude the wind.

This is reason for love. Any fish willing to consort with fishermen on a day when most such meetings are cancelled is worthy of worship.

But there are more dimensions to the barracuda's character, more delights this creature can bestow. More than most other fish, it appears to comprehend the essence of fishing. When, and if, it does take a lure, the barracuda seems to do so after considering each of the options and then saying, "Okay, I will participate in the game." Many times, the fish will indicate quite unmistakably that it does not want to play. Lures twitched within inches of a barracuda's impressive torpedo nose are ignored with the same disdain a senior club member might show for a steward waving a feather duster across a nearby coffee table.

If it is caught by the moment's whimsy, a barracuda may follow a lure, keeping the tip of its toothy, undershot lower jaw less than six inches behind the device at all times,

4

no matter how fast the fisherman retrieves his line. And, when fishing for barracuda, there is no limit to that speed. The faster the lure moves through the water, the more the angler can hope that the barracuda will lose patience and strike it, as if to say, "See, if I'd wanted, I could have sliced you anytime."

Barracudas do not often lose patience. Instead, they follow the lure until it's within a few feet of the angler. If the fisherman is wading, casting in water about crotch deep, he can find himself face to face with a creature who, at that moment, definitely has an advantage. But, contrary to prevailing legend, barracudas do not spend their mornings biting peckers off. After entering the encounter in its daily log of memorable events, the silver fish will turn and disappear.

Its behavior is the same when it follows a lure to a boat drifting across the flats, although there are times when I have looked down at a barracuda an instant before its vanishing act and found its black eyes looking right back. This wondrous and evanescent creature contact most often leaves me certain I could see mischief in those eyes.

On the relatively few occasions when the fish does take a fly, it demonstrates a reckless vitality and will to live that has earned it Jeffrey's love and respect, and the love and respect of every other true fisherman.

As I watch Jeffrey's arm wave against swollen clouds in this unruly February sky, I know he will make his cast after the next arc. Lithe, practiced, and well coordinated, he does not waste time on unnecessary false casts. For him, fly casting is like breathing, a conditioned reflex. And, even in this wind, he has the skills to put the fly pretty much where he wants it within the hundred-foot radius of his potential.

That distance is hedged a bit with barracuda. Their teeth make such short work of most leaders, Jeffrey's fly is tied to four inches of light, stainless-steel braided wire. The lure looks like a pull cut from the drawstring of a whorehouse window-shade. About five inches long, the fly is a lime-green tassel of glitter-flecked synthetic fiber trailing from a blunt head of hard plastic with a hole through its center for the wire leader and attached hook.

This is definitely not a fly for casting in the wind. The tassel spreads, creating resistance, pushing the flyline off its invisible track through space. Once it hits the water and submerges, however, the lure is transformed. Pliant fibers coalesce and become a single, wriggling silver-green tube that emulates a solo, unwary needlefish cruising the flats.

Jeffrey drops the fly about four feet in front of the two dark shadows and starts his retrieve, stripping line quickly with his left hand, moving the lure in rapid spurts away from the fish. He has yanked it halfway to the boat when a shadow moves. One of the barracuda is curious. Jeffrey slows his retrieve for a split second, then begins stripping line as fast he knows how.

"Here he comes," he shouts. "Here he comes."

Moving at half speed now across the white sand, the shadow takes shape, evolves to a three-dimensional force whose intentions are forecast by its tenuous wake rippling in wavering contradiction to the wind's stiff broom. These fluid anomalies, subtle counter-movements in the daily dance of wind and tide, are often the only evidence of life beneath the surface. Just as he reads a channel's evasive patterns on the flats' pale scroll, Jeffrey has also learned to interpret the delicate braille inscribed by fish moving through shoal water.

This barracuda's sentence soon becomes readable even to me. The creature has decided to play, and to win—always to win. What began as traces of feathered water become as prominent as scars on an emerald cheek. Now the fish plows a liquid furrow; if the wind quit its oboe and the short seas stopped slapping at our skiff, we could hear the hiss of this fish's accelerating passage.

It wants the fly. It has determined that this morning it will devour this single, impudent needlefish.

The strike is a gift, the gift a barracuda keeps for its fishermen and always gives with grace. Even though the fish has been seen, even though impending contact has been announced by the creature itself, the meeting has the jolt of a slap on the shins with a two-by-four, the shock of a kick in the groin.

WHAM!

White water geysers on impact. Steely silver whips at the vortex of the strike's instantaneous tumult. Spinning, arcing now away from the boat, this barracuda knows it is betrothed, linked somehow to the skiff's dark shadow by the ersatz deception stuck in its jaw.

Incensed at the trickery, the fish leaps clear, hangs silver thirty feet from the boat, magically aloft, a fierce and scaled prehistoric icon for us to marvel, released from the center of the great stone that is our past, a shimmering miracle released to teach us life.

Then it vanishes into the frothing sea.

And begins its run for freedom.

As taut as the fish he embraces, Jeffrey is tested by the run. Slack line gathered from his cast strips loops along a tossing foredeck, and it is this line the barracuda is claiming as his own. Jeffrey must grant the claim with care. Too quickly given, the line can loop, twine about itself, knot, and stop all passage through the rod's diminishing guides.

This blunder is shortlived, allows no time for correction. The instant the line stops short, the snubbed fish has won, set free by its partner's clumsy violence.

Jeffrey is not given to blunders. Slack line and fish

move in concert, the line flowing through a left hand that maintains a flawless balance of tensions.

Until, at last, after a moment that spans creation, the slack line is taken, the slim rod bows and for the first time Jeffrey feels the heart of the fish beating in his hand.

"He's on the reel," he shouts, delighted at the familiar embrace, the surging, tugging, tossing welcome that throbs from the humming line, along the charged rod, through his arms' arteries to his soul.

Such a generous fish. He gives us his entirety, withholding no thread in the tapestry of his surging repertoire. Water rips like paper in the wake of his dashes across the flats, first this way, now that.

Stops. Runs at us, faster now than Jeffrey can reel. Sensing slack, the barracuda tosses his head high. We see it waving from the whitecaps, shaking with great strength. This fish is still certain it will win.

And Jeffrey knows he will not kill this creature. If no mistakes are made, if this three-foot, fifteen-pound electrifying fish is properly and gracefully played at the end of a slim leader that will break under more than eight pounds of pressure, if indeed the barracuda is brought to boat, he will be released, freed, and, like two lovers parting, both fish and fisherman will have their freedom and their memories.

But while they are coupled, their interactions are as harmonic as a Mozart minuet. There is a kind of precision that must be observed, intricate rhythms to heed. An inept moment, and the fish will end the meeting.

"No," Jeffrey says. "Oh no."

The wind cannot blur the sharp sadness in his voice.

He yanks hard at the rod, violent, cranky motions, so aberrant I am puzzled. It's as if he is trying for the very excess that will surely snap the leader. But why?

I stand, and see.

8

A shark's dorsal rides a dark shape gliding toward our fish. Without haste. Implacable. Almost gentle, like water falling.

Yet there is no gentleness in their meeting.

When the dorsal and Jeffrey's line intersect, the shark's shape emerges. A lemon shark, about seven feet, a tawny submarine beneath its dorsal, wagging now as the shark's head shakes harshly from side to side, convulsively.

Its jaws have closed on the barracuda and the violent side-to-side shaking rips the shark's multiple teeth through the silver fish like a band saw slicing a young pine log. A rusty marigold of blood blossoms to full flower in an instant, a submerged boutonniere on the barracuda's sudden grave.

Turning as deliberately as a bus, the shark glides off fifty feet or so, trying to sense the possible presence of more helpless fodder. Rising from the blood blossom's center, the barracuda's pale head bobs, open black eye staring at us across the water.

Jeffrey reels in limp line, his figure sagging, a weary saddness in his shoulders.

"I saw the shark coming," he says. "I saw it coming and tried to break off the fish." Those were the cranky jerks I had noticed: Jeffrey, trying to snap the leader and set the barracuda free, trying to give it a chance to outswim the shark.

"Too late," he says. Stepping back to the console, he presses the switch that lowers the skiff's 115-horsepower Yamaha outboard shaft so the propellor can get a small bite at the water. Then he starts the engine and steers at the slowest possible speed toward the barracuda head, still floating, still trickling blood into the salt sea.

"See if you can spot my fly," he says as we close the

gap. "The shark must have cut the leader. The fly could be in the barracuda's jaw."

I remember that Jeffrey is the son of a Lithuanian mother and Cuban father, and think to myself that it is his mother's voice I'm hearing. I have heard his father's too, on other days, in other waters, over different fish.

Alongside the severed head, we see no fly, only the barracuda's obsidian eyes staring in relentless reproach.

Jeffrey is fisherman enough to love barracuda. He never wanted this fish to die.

With us through the morning, the wind is not about to take the afternoon off. We are the only skiff on the flats, and the wind is wearing us down.

Jeffrey heads us home, across the chop of Northwest Channel, through the slot east of Wisteria Island where a woman who lives on a sloop moored there is known to sunbathe topless and to wave to passersby. I look as we cruise by her boat; she is not in sight. I look every time, but have never seen her. I believe she will be there, someday.

We slide under the bridge to Fleming Key, along Key West's northern shore and make the turn south at Trumbo Point into Garrison Bight where we slow to trolling speed and throw no wake to jar the hundreds of boats at anchor in this snug harbor.

On our port side as we come from under the Eaton Street bridge are the thirty, forty, and fifty-foot charter boats that take paying customers to the deep waters beyond the reef on Key West's ocean side. High-sided white hulls, flying bridges, fighting chairs, stout rods, spool reels, each waves its outrigger wands at the curious, the afternoon strollers, and the few among them who are considering spending significant bucks on five hours of offshore fishing.

In Key West, any prospect who shows the slightest interest gets a hard sell from the boat's captain, mate, or both.

Which is why every slip is framed by its own open-air

doorway: two sturdy white posts rise about eight feet. The six-foot span at the top is bridged by a plank painted with the boat's name, and often the captain's name and phone number. A foot beneath is another cross-member, this one a stout two-by-six studded with six-inch spikes about four inches apart.

When the returning boats are backed into their slips, engines rumbling, twin screws churning and exhausts burbling, their transoms are directly under the racks. Opening fish boxes, mates toss carcasses onto the dock, hop ashore, hose off the bodies, and pick up the largest by the tail.

Swinging each dead fish like a baseball bat, mates slam the day's trophies against the naked spikes, driving steel through a barracuda's sightless eyes, a sailfish cheek, or dolphin shoulder. There the fish hang, dull, tarnished by the sun, desiccating totems spiked high to validate every captain's come-on: "Hey, the fishing's great!"

Glancing along the line of charter boats as Jeffrey turns west toward the Garrison Bight Marina, I can see the ash-grey carcasses of at least fifteen barracuda, stiff on their spikes. In the evening, when the curious and the passersby and tomorrow's customers have gone, mates will toss the day's detritus back to the sea.

As the sun rises the next morning, if there has been little wind and a gentle tide, the same boats will shoulder aside bleached and bloated bodies of the day before even as skippers set a course for more.

Jeffrey is glum as he eases his boat into her dockside berth. He is remembering how he hoped the day's barracuda would break off in time. He can still see the marigold blossom in the whitecaps.

Today is my sixty-fifth birthday. I am thinking how long it has taken me to begin to comprehend fishing. To begin to see more than a submerged shadow of myself.

I am a slow learner.

11

East Hampton

August 28, 1939

I am the Blanche DuBois of fishermen. I have always depended on the kindness of strangers.

Wyman Aldrich is not a total stranger, but he is in his early sixties and I am sixteen. The two age groups are seldom paired, unless the older is an uncle, grandfather, or guardian; in either case the adolescent involved is likely to be cynical about the chances of finding true happiness with any adult male.

But fishing can change everything, life included.

There is a confluence of elements here on Long Island's East End in late August and early September that creates crystal air. As summer glides toward the autumnal equinox and high pressure builds in the heavens, certain mornings become complete units of hours suspended, as if nature has succeeded in generating a timeless moment, a shimmering souvenir of a passing season, saved and pinned in the book of elements, motionless, perfect, intoxicating, and touched with the tragedy of its own fragility.

This is such a morning. Its glories drape me like

Joseph's coat as I stand at the very edge of the East Hampton Town Dock peering down at schools of silversides, gathered in trembling, emerald circles, throbbing with the panic of their knowledge that they are being watched by this year's crop of adolescent bluefish, the half-pound snappers, already perfect replicas of their savage parents. And, just as those parents slash hapless schools of menhaden to a water-borne melange of blood, guts, and scales, so do these miniatures emulate more massacres. Only the scale differs: instead of dicing one-pound menhaden as their parents do, snappers granulate silversides about as long as my index finger.

As I watch, a silverside school of at least three hundred fish congeals to a sphere as compact as a cannonball. Each individual struggles to find the center of the mass and to stay there, hoping that when a snapper strikes, the outer minnows will be the first to go. The tighter the sphere, the closer their doom. The one I watch is so congealed, I expect it to sink.

From the depths of the Three Mile Harbor channel that flows dark past the dock, a small shape accelerates, aquamarine and silver in the clear waters of this crystal day. Hurtling directly at the silverside sphere, the snapper produces what for him must be a gratifying panic.

The cannonball explodes, becomes an underwater pyrotechnic display as elaborate as any Fourth of July extravaganza. Tiny shooting stars zoom in every direction, filling the underwater sky. Others surface. In concert, on this still morning, the sound of their surfacing is the hiss of a cotton sheet being ripped end to end. Remarkable.

I am fully fascinated. Totally absorbed. Watching fish is, for me, an infallible pastime, more delightful than masturbation, infinitely more enjoyable than tennis lessons, swimming, lunch at the beach, or sailing races at Devon:

each the primary recreational activities our parents, as they continue to remind us, have worked so hard to make possible during our summer holidays on this graceful sandspit between the Sound and the sea 125 miles east of the city where I was born.

Somehow, Wyman Aldrich has recognized my proclivity. Perhaps he and my parents have discussed my odd recreational choice. (I can hear my mother wondering aloud why I'm not on the tennis courts with my friends, or the chosen teenagers she hopes will be my friends.) But although Wyman belongs to the same club, he is not a frequent attender. His wife and my grandmother sit and chat under the awning of Granny's cabana, but Wyman is most often absent.

He has, it turns out, gone fishing.

And somewhere in the course of his nonfishing hours, he has learned I am a fisherman too.

So, on this opalescent forenoon as he pilots his boat past Three Mile's frequent channel markers from her berth at the head of the harbor, he spots me on the Town Dock, fish-watching.

Turning the boat toward the dock, he waves. I return the greeting; I know who he is, but I do not feel that I know him and I wonder if it is I that he approaches. Perhaps, I think, he wants to pick up a lobster or two from Emerson Taber, whose boat and lobster pound occupy the southwest corner of the point of land I'm standing on.

"John," calls Wyman as he gets close enough to be heard over the pop-pop of the one-lung inboard chugging at the center of his sixteen-foot skiff, "come on along. I'm going out in the bay for a little fishing."

How glorious the moment of my acceptance. It is, beyond any doubt, the purest verification of my tenuous independence. The simple, trembling act of clambering

down the pilings to set foot aboard Wyman's waiting boat
is as overpowering for me as Mark Antony's first step
aboard Cleopatra's barge must have been for him.

Wyman's boat is comfortable and complete, decep-
tively simple. From the Town Dock, she appeared to be a
straight-forward skiff: gray, wooden, the sort of open boat
that frequents a thousand harbors. But as I step aboard I
realize this boat is strip-built, and with great care. She is not
a flat-bottomed sharpy banged together over a winter in
some Bonnacker's garage; this boat's bow flares, her curves
flow, and her prim V-bottom is finely fashioned to turn
aside short seas instead of being slapped by them.

Mounted amidships, the one-lung Palmer engine is a
museum piece. Its massive flywheel could anchor a ferry,
and each of its brass petcocks, valves, and fittings are golden
bright in the sun. From stem to stern, everything aboard
this boat is cared for.

Like Wyman. His skin is as tanned and sea-cured as
that of any commercial fisherman. A thin veil of age sifts
the blueness of his eyes, and wrinkles wreathe his neck
where it meets the collar of his open, faded shirt. But his
face—that great, sagging, weatherbeaten, wonderful face—
is alive with Wyman's bright and boyish spirit. I look into
his eyes and there is all the mischief, the excitement, and the
rebellion that I feel as I come aboard: free, gone for the day,
escaped, without even asking or telling anyone where I am
going or who I am with.

"Take a seat," Wyman says, "up forward." He sits in
the stern, steering with a tiller mounted on the gunwale:
push it forward and the boat heads to starboard; pull, and
she turns to port.

Following the narrow channel, we pass the long breakwater of granite blocks, peopled now with fishermen, most
of them with the bamboo poles favored here for snapper

16

fishing. Just add fifteen or twenty feet of line, a snelled hook baited with a silverside, swing it into the tide and soon you can do battle with twelve ounces of scrappy snapper: the best of breakfasts, quickly browned in butter the next morning. Until this adventure, the breakwater has been my only boat. Today I wave to my fellow land-bound anglers as we pass; I am tolerant of the less fortunate.

Past the blinking light at the breakwater's end we turn east, following the shore along Hog Creek inlet, headed for the buoy at Lion's Head Rock where the land corners and falls away to the south, toward Napeague's low dunes, the slim finger of sand that separates the Atlantic from Gardiner's Bay. Where the dunes bend just east of Devon, the smokestacks of the fish-meal factory rise; the channel we follow is deep enough to accommodate the high-bowed, 140-foot bunker steamers that pursue the same menhaden as do the bluefish, net them by the thousands of tons, and steam, gunwales at the water line, to the factory to unload countless flattened fish from their oily holds on conveyors that carry the carcasses to stinking vats where the menhaden are pressed like over-ripe, silver grapes and oil spills from them to be refined to a fine and delicate lubricant.

The squashed remains are loaded into great drying ovens and the flaky residue of bones and flesh ground into fish meal measured into one hundred-pound burlap bags carried, still hot, on the backs of black workers to waiting box cars.

Wyman and I are not thinking of fish as industrial raw material; for us, they are the pivot of our exhilarating freedom and we worship them.

We anchor a few hundred feet off the high, rust-colored cliffs of sand that rise from the shore to the Bell Estate, a place I have never set foot and knew little of until this view from the water. Now I can see the shingled mansion at the

17

cliff's tops, the covered stairway with its electrically powered chair that rides a bannister so visitors to the pier below will not have to make the climb on foot. Mr. Bell, which is all I have ever heard him called, is rich. That much I know. But he has no fishing boat at his dock, and there are rumors that he keeps to himself in the house, tended by a nurse reported to be his mistress.

If I were rich, and lived here, I tell myself, I would fish every day.

Wyman opens several clams, letting juice drip over his fingers, separating the meat from the shells and dropping the flesh into a coffee can he has half-filled with bay water.

"Got these earlier this morning," he says, "near Sammi's Beach. Just waded in and dug them out with my feet. Ever do that, John?"

"No sir," I say, telling myself I'll be sure to try tomorrow.

"There. Now, pass me those two rods and we'll pay a call on Mr. Fish."

I hand Wyman the two stiff, rather stubby, black metal boat-rods. Each is fitted with a Pflueger spool reel loaded with stout Cuttyhunk line ending in a stiff gut leader made fast to two hooks, one above the other, and a four-ounce, pyramid, lead sinker.

Taking a slice of raw clam from the coffee can, Wyman threads it onto one of the hooks. "Put some of this foot meat on," he explains. "It's tough, hard to steal.

"Then, on the other, we'll give those fish plenty of gooslum. Take this juicy stuff here, this part that runs along the edge of the shell, and hook it through a couple of times at one end." His brown, blunt fingers caress a flimsy strand of clam that reminds me of what I find in my handkerchief after I sneeze.

"There," he says. "See how that gooslum hangs off the

18

hook. In the water, that behaves like a worm wriggling. A worm, or maybe a sand eel. Fish just love it.

"Here." He hands me a rod with both hooks baited.

"Drop the line down until you feel the sinker hit bottom, then reel in just enough so the sinker bumps when you move your rod tip up and down."

Tentatively, eyeing Wyman as he works his rod, I release the reel's brake. The bottom seems a long, dark ways down as line slips through the guides. I try to imagine how the bait looks now that it has left the sunlight to swim in the invisible mystery so far beneath us.

Bump. I feel a soft thud along the rod as tension leaves the line. Wyman, who is watching, says, "That's bottom. Now reel in just a bit. Get the line tight.

"Ahh," he says after a minute or so, "there's Mr. Fish. A touch. I have a touch, and another." He laughs.

I think to myself, he must have dropped his line right on top of a fish.

But Wyman is not moving his hands. He sits there, intent, his eyes on the moving tip of his rod, bowing now, bending just a bit.

Wyman grunts as the tip bends sharply; then he rares back, lifting the rod much more vigorously than I expected.

"Well, hello there," he says. "Hello, hello, hello."

He is turning the crank handle on his reel, retrieving line slowly, steadily, enjoying every moment, laughing, savoring for surely the thousandth time this summer, this first meeting of the day with his friend, the fish, a friend he talks to throughout their acquaintance.

"Come on, now, don't leave me now, not without a look. I know you're not too big, but you could make a nice meal. And I want John to see you. You don't feel like a flounder, not like a weakfish. I think I know what you are. Yes, I do. I think I know you, Mr. Fish.

19

"Well bless my soul," says Wyman, as he lifts up his rod and swings a small, brown-and-white grotesque dumpling of a fish into the boat. "You're a blowfish. A blowfish.

"Ever meet Mr. Blowfish, John?"

I shake my head, staring at the creature.

Picking it up, holding it in his hand like a potato, Wyman wiggles the hook free, carefully. He pushes the fish toward me. "Here, look here," he says, pointing at the strange, small face peering from the circle of Wyman's fingers and thumb.

"Pay attention to these teeth, John. These are teeth that bite, and they are strong enough to do damage." I see four teeth, two up, two down. They look like the teeth cartoonists put in chipmunk's mouths: flat, wide, curved just a bit. Teeth for a rodent, not a fish.

"And look at these eyes. A blowfish has green eyes. Can you believe it."

The eyes I see are almond-shaped, almost oblong, set close above what ought to be a blowfish nose, even though I know fish don't have noses. But this one has no gills, not that I can see. This fish appears to be all head, with a shape like a foreshortened, mottled, brown eggplant, with four teeth and two green eyes at the fat end, and a tapering, short body that ends in a flimsy tail flapping aimlessly against Wyman's wrist.

"Watch this, John."

Turning the blowfish over, Wyman reveals its white belly, a white so pale it is luminous. With his index finger, he scratches the belly, gently, almost a tickle. Making sounds I never anticipated, short grunts and grinding of those teeth, the blowfish begins to swell. First, its belly, like a large blister, then the entire body inflates, taut, rigid, under internal pressures that startle me. The skin that seemed almost slimy when the blowfish came from the water has been transformed; now it is rough, bristling with a thousand tiny spines that are coarse sandpaper on my fingertips as I rub the pale belly.

What Wyman holds is no longer a fish, but a near-perfect sphere, a large grapefruit with a tummy taut enough to drum. Heaving the softball into the air, Wyman laughs as the creature arcs against our perfect autumnal sky.

When it hits the water, the blowfish floats for a split second, a small buoy in the channel. Then, with a quick burble, it deflates and is gone.

"Too small to keep," Wyman says. "But his big brothers and sisters are still down there. You better check your line, John. You haven't been paying attention to your fishing."

He's right. When I reel in, both my hooks are bare.

We catch six keepers in the next half hour, throw back as many small ones. It's all blowfish today; no weakfish, no fluke, not even a skate.

Wyman asks, "Want some lunch?" I say yes and wait for him to reach into one of his knapsacks for a sandwich or crackers, but he asks me to haul in the anchor and when I do he starts the Palmer and heads for Cartwright Shoal.

About a mile to the east of our fishing spot, Cartwright is little more than a large sandbar just high enough above water to allow beach grass to get a grip. Separated from Gardiner's Island by a shoal and turbulent channel not more than a half-mile wide, Cartwright was probably part of the island a thousand years ago. Some treasure hunters are certain it was; they claim Captain Kidd buried a good part of his loot somewhere on Gardiner's, and they say Cartwright is one of the most likely spots. No treasure has ever been found, but over at the fish factory store where oil coats, hooks, tarred line, and boots are sold to commercial fishermen, there is plenty of talk about gill netters and trap fishermen who have found gold coins in the Cartwright sand.

To my knowledge, no one has ever seen an actual coin on display, however.

Like two pirates, Wyman and I wade ashore after he nudges the bow of his skiff into soft sand on Cartwright's south shore. We carry equipment and supplies Wyman pulled from the cuddy as we neared the island: a wire grill, knife, bread board, skillet, two bottles of ginger ale, and a small slab of salt pork wrapped in waxed paper. I decide there's no guessing how much stuff Wyman has packed into that small space under the forward deck.

After we get organized, I go back to the skiff for the bucket that holds the blowfish. Wyman has already started a small fire built from the driftwood that litters much of Cartwright.

Taking one blowfish at a time from the bucket, he holds it belly down on the bread board and makes a deep cut behind its head. Then he works his thumb under the skin of the back half, holds tight to the head, and yanks the skin from the whole rear part of the fish. A tapering, pearly chunk of meat emerges, as innocent as a newborn. It's about four inches long and I would never have guessed such an odd-looking fish could give birth to such a morsel.

Wyman puts the six pearls into the hot skillet, already popping with a couple of chunks of salt pork, tosses some pepper, and keeps the morsels moving with his knife blade. Meanwhile, herring gulls are having a screaming time of it with the blowfish guts and heads we left for them at the water's edge.

Every moment of this pageant of preparation is new to me. Never before have I seen fish caught, cleaned, and cooked within an hour. Never before have I smelled the magic of salt pork in a frying pan over an open fire flickering on a pirate island where we are the only two humans for miles. Wyman Aldrich has made this possible. He is supposed to be having lunch by the club pool with his wife and my grandmother; they are there at this moment, shaking their heads at the old man's ornery independence. I decide then and there that Wyman Aldrich is my hero, the person I want to become. For this day he has raised the curtain on a watery stage set with wonders, wonders that wait for me.

Sitting here on an ancient ship's timber too heavy for anything but a hurricane to have brought to Cartwright, pushing hot flakes of sweet and fragrant white, fresh fish into my mouth, tasting the salt pork's tang and relishing the woodsmoke on the enchanted equinoctial air, I know with infinite certainty that I have found the fulcrum of my future. A boat, a fishing rod and reel, and the knowledge to guide me to the fullest realization of their potential for adventure—this is what life holds for me, out there in the coming of age that I have, until this day, viewed with such skeptical anxiety.

Sweeping from horizon to horizon is the setting of my years, caught here in the piercing clarity of this instant: Montauk Point off to the northeast, Hither Hills rising dark to the east, Napeague's slim fingers of sand, the pushing stacks of the fish factory, the white pickets of the yacht club dock, Bell's mansion on the rusty cliffs, Lion Head Rock, and off to the northwest, the smudge of Connecticut across the Sound, blending with Fisher's Island and pulling in to the green woods of Gardiner's Island just over my shoulder. I am surrounded by the salt sea and the land that frames it in this magnificent meeting of the two. Today, the world spins about me waiting to take me aboard.

When Wyman unloads me back at the Town Dock in the weighty silence of a still mid-afternoon, I have no words of proper gratitude. What can I tell him? I can barely cope with the massive import of the day's unfolding. There are such moments: even in the midst of my clumsy, fumbling, pubescent years I perceive the worth of this August episode. I know, I truly do know as I wave to Wyman, standing, steering up the channel in the stern of his skiff with the sun over his shoulder, that he has, this day, given me a gift whose dimensions will take a lifetime to decipher.

And, incredibly, my day is not over.

In the evening the older sister of a summer neighbor down the road telephones. She may be, for all I know, eighteen or even more. She has her own car, but we have scarcely spoken through the summer; she was there, that's all, when my brother Chick and I went to visit her younger brother, for touch football, or a bike ride to the village where we would sit at the White's Drug Store soda fountain assuaging our adolescence with sundaes swathed in chocolate and topped with powdered malted milk. "Dustys," we called them.

"Come on over," she says. "I'm all alone. Ned is off to school and my parents are in town."

It is dusk as I ride my bike the quarter mile along Apaquogue Road to the place her parents rent for the summer. My heart is a pheasant beating short wings against my chest; my mouth is dry as powdered malted milk. What does she want? What is expected of me? What is not expected of me?

She, on the other hand, is absolutely in control. There is a smile in her eyes, a perfect equanimity in every comment. Jesus, she is old. Tall, in a white, pleated linen skirt with a cashmere sweater across her shoulders, her dark hair and blue eyes swimming over crimsoned lips against her summer-tanned cheeks, she says, "Let's go for a ride."

It is her own car, a maroon Ford coupe. She is the only

girl I know with her own car, and I don't suppose I really know her.

She drives east, through the village, past Amagansett, on to the Montauk Highway as the night spins by us under cold stars hung from a moonless sky. From the highest of the Hither Hills I can look northwest and see the pale sheet of Gardiner's Bay unfolding toward Connecticut; I am looking at the very seascape of the day's discoveries. It is this air, I tell myself, this electric equinoctial air. I am under a spell, lifted into the pages of a book more compelling than any I have ever read.

When we reach the Montauk Light, she prowls the parking lots until we find a place that overlooks the Atlantic and the Sound, that turbulent meeting place of perpetual tides.

But no more turbulent than our encounter. Enfolding me against her cashmere, she presses her lips to mine. Her tongue is a hot, darting sand eel, exploring every cavern of my esophagus, wriggling, alive inside me.

This is a first. I am electrified, jolted, slammed without pity into an encounter with passion. Stunned, totally stunned, motionless, I cannot respond, not for a while.

Then, as the blowfish in my corduroys swells to the rigidity of structural steel, I ask my own cruller of a tongue to try to catch up with the sand eel swimming in my mouth. My hands fumble aimlessly at cashmere.

Perhaps it is twenty minutes, even half an hour, before she ends the exercise. For me, it is an eternity. But she pulls back, as coolly as if she were changing courts in a tennis match, turns the ignition key, steps on the starter, and off we roll toward home.

No matter how I fashion my halting words, I cannot find the formula that will extend the evening. "Good night,

Johnny," she says as we stand at her door. "I've got to get some sleep. Tomorrow morning I leave for the city."

I ease aching loins aboard my bike and pedal home, pondering the miracles this day has wrought.

No girl ever called me "Johnny" before.

But I go to sleep remembering Wyman.

East Hampton

August 11, 1956

Next to the hefty, creosoted pilings of the Town Dock, Marshall looks so small I wonder if I should have brought him here. Standing on his little bed at home, his blond hair tossing above his wide, brown eyes as he puts up his arms so I can hoist him to mine, he seems almost a young adult. And the solid weight of him against my chest surprises me. Soon, I realize, our son will not be so easy to carry around.

But even with my finger crooked through the suspenders that hold up his summer shorts, I worry. A three-year-old ought not to be so close to the dock's edge, a single, short step from Three Mile Harbor's deep channel and swift tides. Yet there is no other way he can catch his first fish: an accomplishment I have wanted for him since he was born at the Southampton Hospital on the first day of spring.

Snappers, I decide, will be the perfect inaugural. They take the hook, need no provocation other than the presence of a silverside, and strike with such abandon that no technique is required from the fisherman. So Marshall, his bare back and shoulders bronzed by a summer outdoors and at the beach, stands at the dock's edge holding a bamboo pole in his hands.

"Watch the bobber," I tell him, pointing to the small red-and-white plastic ball attached to his line about three feet above the baited hook. "You have to pull up on the pole when you see the bobber go under. There are fish down there. See, the splash, there. And there."

How right, I think, that we are at the Town Dock. So many of my fishing days have started here; now, our first-born son begins his.

Looking across the channel, I can conjure Wyman in his skiff, chugging toward me, coming to carry me to other worlds. We met here many times during the months before the war, a war that thundered toward me in silence. I was blessed with incredible innocence and ignorance of the world beyond my summers, even though my mother was in Austria and escaped with Buffy Harkness, lying on the floor of Buffy's Rolls hidden under lap robes while her chauffeur lied to guards at the Swiss border. Perhaps Wyman heard about the incident, but he never mentioned it, or the war.

Flounder, bluefish, weakfish, fluke, skate, and more blowfish—together, Wyman and I caught them all. And on a mid-September afternoon, my last before college, we took several hand-carved plover decoys to Gull Island, the sand bar just across the channel from the Town Dock, and set them out along the shore. We made a rough blind from beach grass and a driftwood log and sat half-hidden there while Wyman floated a liquid, whistling call on the languid air—a plover call, as perfect as that from any of the birds.

From their trembling, restless flocks gathering for their two-thousand-mile migration, black-bellied plover turned, wheeled in the tender September sunlight, and set down as gently as dandelion seeds among Wyman's decoys.

"We used to hunt them, you know," he said to me, reliving through me and the birds the evenings of his boyhood when still-warm plover, as light as air, bled in his hand.

After the war, after the blood of our bombadier swelled in my hands, I visited Wyman in Palm Beach where he wintered modestly. Just as our first trip to Cartwright forever shaped my daydreams, my Indian River voyages in Wyman's skiff left me indelibly marked by Florida's dramatic contrasts.

On the river, sliding along the soft water, feeling the sweet, soft air on my cheeks, rolling in the satin warmth of those sub-tropical temptations, and comprehending the wonder of the weather's year-round benevolence, I knew that somewhere in the future of what was then a bewildered life that I would return to this bizarre peninsula where men have done their damnedest to destroy nature, but where natural presences still maintain in some places, and dominate wherever there is open water.

Oh, that water. The water that Wyman showed me first. The tepid, creamy seas on the ocean side where pompano swam along the blades of waves. Digging fast in the fine, compacted coral sand, we would finger sand crabs from their holes, force a hook through their hard shells and, without even a rod, twirl a weighted line around our heads like a bolo and toss it just behind the surf.

Once in a great while, like lightning in winter, one of the gun-metal and sapphire, round, powerful fish would take the crab and I would be fast to a kite tossed by an underwater wind, pushing first this way and then that, tugging at the bare line in my salty palms. If we landed a fish, we would take it back to Wyman's small house on the Indian River side and cook it that evening for supper. I have

29

never eaten pompano as good since, and have quit trying to find any.

We fished together for trout—the weakfish relative they call trout in south Florida—the last time I ever saw Wyman. Afternoon on the Indian River, in the same skiff that took us to Cartwright, carried carefully on a truck to Palm Beach so Wyman would never be friendless even when he fished alone, and today I am here. We drift and cast shrimp-baited hooks toward the dark banks and under trees where eagles wait, their heads pale torches in the pines. Wyman has a strike, a big fish, he tells me, taking line, forcing a deep bow in his slim rod. Paddling the skiff, I try to keep Wyman facing his fish as we shift here and there on the river, hoping to keep contact. Sweat gathers on Wyman's brow, drips into his animated eyes and joyful smile. This is bliss. Then the fish is gone, with no goodbye, just gone, finning easily into its mystery as Wyman's shoulders sag. But not for long. "That was so fine," he says, and we go home. I see the setting sun glow on the brown, mottled backs of his strong, tawny hands as he ties up his skiff for the night. I see them still.

Gull Island sits on Marshall's small shoulder as I kneel behind him looking across the harbor, listening for a plover's call, watching the red-and-white bobber twitching below us on the dark tide.

Then it is not there.

Yanked from below with a ferocity that always surprises me, the bobber vanishes. Marshall is motionless, startled by the invisible force that bows the bamboo in his hands.

"Lift. Lift," I tell him, hardly able to keep from taking the rod, pulling with every psychic fiber to get Marshall started. And lift he does, hesitating at first, wondering if

30

there is supposed to be resistance, uncertain if he should contest it. But not a bit uncertain of the urgency in my voice.

Stand-off. For an endless moment, Marshall leans, trying to lift; the fish pulls, fighting for life.

I marvel at the force of the snapper's struggle. A tiny creature on nature's scale, not yet a pound, has convinced a three-year-old of the power of its presence.

Then Marshall gains ground. The rod tip rises, line climbs from the water, and soon the fish is there, on the surface, skittering, flashing blue-green and silver.

Once it leaves the water, it weighs more on the hook and Marshall's lofting slows. He is laughing now that he can see the fish, laughing and on his way to dropping everything: bamboo pole, bobber, line, hook, and snapper blue.

But I am still hollering, and the boy responds. The fish flops at his feet on the Town Dock gravel.

"Your first fish," I shout. Marshall smiles.

We get in the car. The fish is in a bucket in the back seat where Marshall can see it from his harness.

I would, I think on the way home, take Marshall blow-fishing next, if there were any blowfish left in the bay. A few years after that day on Cartwright, someone from General Foods discovered the same pale nuggets. Blowfish fillets became "Chicken of the Sea," packaged and frozen and sold in stores as far away as San Diego. Fish traps along Gardiner's Bay shores bulged with the bounty once a nuisance, and after a few years blowfish were no longer plentiful. By the time Marshall turned three, they were scarce.

After supper, Marshall goes to the refrigerator and reaches for his fish. Holding it close, he takes it with him to his bed where it spends the entire night.

Key West

March 23, 1987

From mid-January through the end of March, this is a city of tensions. Too many humans of too many different sorts crowd this small island. There is not room enough within this hummock's three-mile length and its two-mile width to cope with thousands of day-trippers from Miami, Lauderdale, and West Palm, more thousands of students on their so-called spring breaks that span the seasons from New Year's to Memorial Day, the resident homosexuals and their visiting friends, Key West's business community making certain that each of these numbered days produces its projected profits or more, the neutral natives, ex-Navy, retired insurance executives from Rahway and Albany, and the small army of laborers in this overgrown tropic vineyard: waiters and waitresses, desk clerks and short-order cooks, supermarket checkout cashiers, taxi drivers, bartenders, bouncers, guitar players, and undercover cops making daily drug busts.

As if this mix lacked explosive potential, cruise ships call more and more frequently, disgorging cargoes of hundreds of men and women, all of them dressed in polyester shirts and shorts, carrying their maps as they roam Duval Street looking for the romance they were told they would surely discover here in this home of Hemingway and Williams, this last resort, this Conch Republic that makes rebellion just enough of a reality to thrill visitors from Cleveland and Des Moines.

Too many expectations are raised, too many hopes ignited for this fundamentally funky place ever to fulfill. And there is the weather. Here where two seas meet, where the Gulf and the Atlantic become such restless partners, the weather is seldom stable. These are not the arid realms of southern Arizona where vast reaches of alkali maintain, holding elemental certainty within their static grasp. Here seas surge in an eternity of turbulence, uneasy couplers bickering across the tides, unable to find surcease or slumber.

What may appear to be a peaceful dawn can churn to near darkness by mid-morning. Lauderdale ladies rubbing sun-block on cellulite thighs as they wait on Smathers Beach to catch the rays are roused from their sprawls by a chill wind from the east, sent back to their rooms at the Quality Inn by great, greasy clouds low enough to shine the streets with the sheen of their unwelcome mists.

Winds regroup, restored by the energies of tumbling Carribbean currents that mix cold waters with warm, poke thermal fingers into a vapid sky, stirring small gales that slap at Key West first, stinging the cheeks of strollers on the White Street pier, sending seas thumping at bulkheads, surging along storm drains and surfacing in salt geysers through Duval Street grates, flooding Old Town avenues, dousing rental cars in brine and souring the short-lived high spirits of thousands of ignorant visitors denied their promised sun.

Surliness rules. Women migrate toward the shops,

34

flicking merchandise off counters at Fast Buck Freddie's, trying on Birkenstocks, rattling antique teacups at the China Clipper, but seldom buying, turning instead from the merchandise toward the dripping out of doors, watching bitterly for the blue-sky signal of their reprieve.

Meanwhile, men gather in bars, shaking salt into their beers to wash away the remnants of a morning at Mel Fisher's Museum, or ordering up iced rum concoctions to verify the authenticity of their tropic holidays. Sodden by dinner, they will grumble about the check at La Te Da and promise themselves that next year they will never leave Disneyland.

Some of us, however, go fishing.

My brother, Chick, and his wife are here in Key West, staying at a guest house off Eaton Street, wondering if they should try a swim in the pool, even though the sky has been as gray as slate since first light.

Jeffrey has a half-day charter for the morning, and we will meet him at Garrison Bight at one for an afternoon on the flats. A teacher at Pomfret School, Chick is on his own spring break, and Ceci is taking a holiday from selling real estate in northwestern Connecticut, one of New England's hottest markets.

She does not want to fish. Chick, ever agreeable, always cheerful, perpetually optimistic, welcomes every experience. He has been a painter since boyhood, still paints every day, a remarkable testimony to his unquenchable spirit. So he will fish with me cheerfully because he knows I want to go and because he excludes no possibilities.

He has, however, never been a fisherman. Except for John Graves, our Texas brother-in-law, I am the only committed angler in the family. After catching his first snapper at three and raising my hopes for a fishing son, Marshall began racing motorcycles at fifteen and became a first-rate mechanical engineer with a good job in Portland, Maine, where he has built his own go-kart that he races on weekends.

Calibrated on Jeffrey's receivers, this afternoon's gray weather sends a message quite different from the one that drives so many women into the shops and moves their men to the bars. Jeffrey has been on the water most of his life. At thirteen, almost twenty years ago, he set sail alone from his then home in Fort Lauderdale in a twelve-foot Telstar he named *Cutty Shark*. A runaway, like Huck Finn, Jeffrey made the trip through the Everglades and backcountry, a near wilderness he shared with hippies met on deserted islands, fish caught on the flats, and all the weather south Florida could generate, including a lightning storm that had him shivering alone in a hammock strung between two mangrove trees on some nameless Everglades hummock. It was that night, according to Jeffrey, that he was visited by the great skunk ape of the Glades, sub-tropic brother of the Himalayas' Abominable Snowman.

Nine years later, he crossed the Atlantic alone in his twenty-three-foot sloop, chatting many mornings with the small school of dolphin that sailed with him much of that long and solitary voyage.

Weather, for a man who has seen the south Florida heavens torn by midnight lightning over his open-air hammock, or watched the implacable mountains of the Atlantic's gale-powered swells steamroll toward his small sloop, is always relative. Today's wind is impolite, but not unlivable. This afternoon's sodden skies may make it more difficult to see fish on the flats, but it does not mean the fish have abandoned their homes.

When Chick and I arrive at Garrison Bight, Jeffrey is waiting in his boat, *Waterlight,* the second of the flats boats he has owned since he began guiding—this one a seventeen-foot Mako fitted with a poling platform above its stern transom, a center control console, and a forward casting deck free of cleats and catches. An able boat with a modified "V" hull, its high sides and considerable weight make it more difficult to pole than many other flats boats and Jeffrey talks now and then about selling this *Waterlight* and buying a better new one, maybe even a Maverick like Gil Drake's.

"Everybody set?" he asks as *Waterlight* clears the harbor at Trumbo Point. "We're going to get up on a plane."

Standing behind us at the console, Jeffrey pushes forward on the throttle, accelerating to just under maximum speed. Side by side in front of him, seated like two schoolboys on the same small bench, Chick and I feel the wind shove at our faces as the boat quickly picks up speed. Her bow rises, rises, then drops as her hull shakes free of the water's surface tension. Now only the stern quarter and the prop are in contact with the sea; at thirty-five knots we seem closer to flying than boating.

We head almost due north, toward the Bay Keys and the flats west of them. The keys, and the Lower Harbor Keys to their east, will give us some shelter from a northeast wind that seems determined to keep fishing with us.

Several hundred feet from the flats he wants to work, Jeffrey shuts down the Yamaha, clambers to the poling platform, and picks up the twenty-foot fiberglass pole with a point at one end and a short, two-pronged fork at the other. For the rest of our time on this flat, Jeffrey's arms, shoulders, and skills will provide the energy that makes our hunt possible.

It has taken us less than twenty minutes to make the trip from Trumbo Point to what Jeffrey calls the Back Country, yet we have traveled from one world to another. On the southeast horizon, I can see the tall smokestack rising from the City Electric generating unit at the north end of Grinnell Street where Key West Bight bends into a snug harbor where shrimp boats take shelter from winter storms, jammed bow-to-stern in a welter of wheelhouses and rigging so thick it blocks the sky. One block south of the stack, chefs and waiters and bartenders are getting set for a frantic evening at Dickie's, fastening plastic sheets along the sides of the restaurant patio to keep wind and rain from spoiling the evening for diners from Dayton and Philadelphia. And on Caroline Street, braless college girls in T-shirts bike to the Raw Bar for conch fritters and a beer.

But if I look north, away from the skyline of funk, hard sell, laid back, tropical, human triple-decker of Key West, I look to a wilderness. This is the incredible contrast of the place, the regal presence of natural splendors on the doorstep of a bed and breakfast island. Fifteen minutes from the Quality Inn, we are in a place where we need to be careful if we are to survive.

The contrast exhilarates me, thrills me with its affirmations of natural persistence. Drag lines may have scarred South Florida for life, and cigar butts tossed by Manhattan's refugees may clog Miami's storm drains, but this vital, sinuous, thriving, often impassable wilderness of flats and mangroves and dubious channels spills northeast 125 miles to Florida's marshy mainland fringes, and seventy miles southwest to the quite useless brick and bare ground of Fort Jefferson, built on Garden Key more than a century ago to protect the Keys against a military enemy who never arrived.

It was men and women in short-sleeved shirts and sandals who came instead and proved themselves more destructive than any armada Cortez ever commanded. But even vast armies from the north could not devise strategies for defeating the wilderness of the flats and their hummocks sculpted by winds of eons, great clenched fists of mangrove roots curled in death grips around heads of living coral.

By the time technologies may have been devised to loosen the mangrove's clasp, a few enlightened men and women in Florida and Washington began to comprehend the potential for disaster and built bureaucratic barriers to defend much of this fascinating, shallow-water world. The U.S. Department of Interior regulates and protects what is surely the largest submerged wildland in the world, the necklace of keys and hummocks that unfolds west of Key West to the Marquesas and beyond. This flat we fish today is part of the Great White Heron National Wildlife Refuge, and I give vast thanks for that, for every Nat Reed and Marjorie Stoneman Douglas who ever went to the mat for tarpon, herons, mangroves, turtle grass, and each of the other bright links in the vast ecological chain that keeps truth rooted here just minutes from a Florida coast that is a colossus of prevarication, of condos standing on sand dredged from beneath the very place where more condos will rise.

For me, Key West is about its water wilderness. For granting this access, I can forgive this seedy island city its every excess, and treasure its considerable contentments: the high fires of poinciana in May, the extravagance of bougainvillea blooms each and every day, and the warmth of an airborne sea that washes through open windows as I rest, reminding me that in fifteen minutes a boat can carry me to a world that exists here and nowhere else. I could, I know, spend the rest of all my years reading the flats pale scrolls, and awake each dawn eager for yet another marvelous page.

Since we first met, Jeffrey has been my librarian. It is he who knows where the flats records are kept. Without him and his insights, Chick and I would be drinking in some bar, wondering why so many others have, like us, traveled all the way to Key West if all they wanted was a beer.

Instead, we are here, aboard the *Waterlight*, awash in our solitude, the three of us alone on this small boat, adrift in eighteen inches of salt water so clear that were it not for the wind and clouds, we could read even the fine print of the pages written on marl punctuated with points of undulating turtle grass.

Jeffrey bends to his pole, using the skills of his years to move the skiff cross wind. Beneath his cap's visor, behind the polarized lenses of his dark glass, his sea-green eyes probe the wind-wrinkled surface for signs of fish: barracuda, permit, shark, mutton snapper, perhaps even a tarpon, if one of those great silver fish strays from the channel onto the flats, unlikely this early in the year.

Standing on the bow's flat casting platform, Chick holds a spin-casting rod, its reel loaded with eight-pound-test monofilament. Casting downwind as much as possible, he gets great distance, helped by the weight of the tube lure Jeffrey hopes will entice barracuda. Lime-green, plastic, surgical tubing strung on stainless-steel wire, with a hook near its middle and another near its tail, this is the universal deception for everyone who baitcasts or trolls for barracuda. Bunched just a bit on its wire spine, so the tube bends slightly, the lure "swims" through the water if and when it's retrieved quickly enough. After two or three strikes, the tubing is shredded by the barracuda's teeth. On days when his charters fish for 'cuda the entire trip, Jeffrey may discard as many as fifteen lacerated lures, and spend the evening making as many new ones at his home on Catholic Lane.

With the wind unwilling to grant us much visibility and gray clouds pushing ever closer from above, even Jeffrey finds it almost impossible to see fish resting in the pale circles of white marl that bloom here and there on the bottom. So Chick casts "blind," tossing the tube lure in a pattern that fans from one quarter to another as the boat slips silently across this vast, underwater garden where sponges blossom and needlefish take wing.

Properly done, spin-casting is not tiring; the rod is designed to do the work if a caster lets it. At sixty-three, Chick is still trim, the athlete he has been since our boyhood together. At Pomfret, he coaches one of the crews and prides himself on the spring still in his legs, the wiry resilience of his well-muscled arms. His casts, even though he has done little fishing like this, are easy; he is covering the ground.

He hooks and lands a small barracuda; both the fish and Chick do their best to enliven the brief encounter, but the contest is foregone and shortlived. Jeffrey releases the feisty juvenile, who vanishes with a wave of its broad tail.

"This is slow fishing," Jeffrey says, "and it will likely stay slow as long as this wind holds and the sun doesn't shine. What shall we do?" He looks at us, a smile widening under his sandy mustache. He knows we have no answer, and I am certain he knows we won't ask him to head home.

"There are a few tarpon moving in the channels," he says. "We could give them a try."

I have seen tarpon slide with the grace of a glider under the lights of the Pier House deck where it juts into the Key West Harbor channel across from Tank Island. Dinner guests at the waterfront hotel toss crackers and bread crusts to smaller fish attracted by the submerged spots David Wolkowsky had installed when he designed the first of Key West's luxury accommodations. Jack, blue runners, snappers, goatfish, grunts, and an occasional parrot fish are regular visitors. Some evenings, barracuda hang just at the edge of the shadows, waiting, as they seem to do so often,

41

motionless, ruminating, I suppose, on which of the careless they will claim.

Then, every so often, from the blue-black dark of the channel, a great silver shape will glide as gently as if it were inflated and borne on undersea air currents. Such a delicate entrance for a 150-pound fish more than six feet long. It turns like a dancer whose feet never touch the stage and disappears in the dark again, leaving behind the rattle of surprised chatter along the Pier House rail, where children are calling to their parents to come and see the big fish.

To me, tarpon are more than big. More than any child, I have hung over the deck rail watching and waiting for a silver presence to appear—a vision from the darkness of night waters. And each time the creature materializes in the field of underwater light, I am struck by its grace, the fine dignity of its passage. No tail flips, no excited, sudden muscular movements, not even the quivering suspension of one of the smaller fish as it tries to hold its place in the gathering of its brethren. I am quite the master of my element: that's the statement every tarpon verifies with its sweet turnings.

And now Jeffrey says we may have a chance to meet one.

As February's days edge toward the earlier sunrises of March, they bring the vanguard of the spring tarpon armies that will migrate from the ocean to the Gulf. Solitary fish thread the channels, feeding, moving, keeping to the depths. V-bottomed launches with plenty of room in their sterns anchor in the center of the dark-blue waterways. Their captains trade with shrimp boat skippers: a case of beer for a tub of shrimp, and pink tidbits are ladled into the tide to become a river of chum, bits of shrimp drifting like fallen leaves through the sea's supple air.

Gliding, weightless on the channel's currents, tarpon bless each shrimp, taking each morsel without effort, turning first this way, then that, offering the last rites as graciously as a bishop, inhaling, with dignity and without haste, the seaborne bounty brought their way. Until one great fish inhales the single shrimp in the entire procession that wears a stainless-steel hook through its back.

Then, if the hook holds in the hard mouth, the tarpon is fast to heavy line, a sturdy boat rod, and, in all too many cases, an angler who has come up with $350 for the day and wants a dead fish to show for it. Captains of these bait-fishing boats equip their anchors with quick-release buoys; within seconds after the fish is hooked, the boat joins the angler, becomes an ally in the battle, moving where the tarpon moves, minimizing the few skills required to keep a fish on sixty-pound-test line and a rod that could haul a Volkswagon from the bottom.

More often than the anglers like to admit, once the carcass is dockside and the $500 mounting fee becomes a reality, Project Over-the-Fireplace is abandoned and the body dumped into the waters it was taken from a few hours earlier. This time, however, there is no graceful surge of goodbye. Instead, the blanched mass of the carcass drifts from one side of the harbor to another, a waterborne albatross around the charter industry's neck.

Several bait-fishing boats are still anchored in Northwest Channel as we approach. Jeffrey carefully keeps his distance, making certain the *Waterlight* is no disruption to anyone's fishing. In the late-afternoon light, the sky and its companion sea are darker now, somber, leaden, with both clouds and whitecaps beating faster in the boisterous northeaster.

Fifty feet off our beam, rising pewter from dun swells, sighing like the wind, six tarpon roll. It's as if the restless waters parted, exposing these secret voyagers in the midst of their journey. Then, like porpoise, tarpon heads go down, long backs arch, and the fish are gone, a vision vanished from the sight of some demented desert traveler.

Five minutes later, the waters part once more, this time astern.

From my perch on the bow, I cast a compact plastic plug, a traditional red-headed, white-bodied lure used by casters of artificial bait the world over for freshwater and saltwater fish of all sorts and sizes. This one is about the size a light-tackle Jersey surfcaster would offer a bluefish.

Cast and retrieve. Cast and retrieve. Cast and retrieve. The process is repetitive but never boring, not after I have seen fish with my own two eyes. As long as this proof of their presence burns in my brain, I could cast until midnight.

But no such endurance is needed.

Retrieving, winding the ten-pound-test monofilament slowly onto the open-faced spinning reel, stopping now, then yanking and reeling, I feel resistance, as if the three-ounce lure has tangled with a strand of seaweed. I jerk it free, but feel the rod bend in my hand.

Then, like Athena leaping from the cloven head of Zeus, the waters part and the entire monument of a six-foot tarpon rises erect, complete, a silver obelisk mounted on a heaving sea. For a long moment I am convinced there is no connection. He is a fish sent to terrify me with his awesome presence; I am retrieving a plug cast sterile upon the waves.

Yet the rod bends as the leap begins. Shock has stolen my breath, I cannot move. It is the weight of the line itself and its reluctance to leave the water as the fish reaches for the clouds that sets the hook, not my retarded reflexes.

"He's on!" Jeffrey shouts. "He's on!"

By now, I agree. Tumbling back to the bumpy sea, the tarpon crashes in a welter of white water, vanishes, and leaves me staring at a reel losing its line faster than any I have seen. After a few seconds, I am convinced there will be only this: my head bent in startled study as two hundred yards of line is taken from me by a force I cannot comprehend, even though I have recorded the image of that leap on memory's slate forever.

"He's coming up," yells Jeffrey, who has been watching the line, me, Chick, the boat, the other boats, and, with his seventh sense, the fish I cannot see.

Again the tarpon leaps. This time not quite clear of the surface, but so far from us that for the second time I am convinced we are separate, the fish in his world now, I in mine.

But we are linked, still.

"Now he's rushing the boat. Reel, John. Reel as fast as you can. Faster than you've ever reeled." Jeffrey's words are urgent, and I try, cranking the reel's small handle until my wrist aches. I find time to wonder: how did I get involved in such a meeting? It is raining now, hard. The wind punches the channel to ever larger lumps, bucking the boat beneath me. And I am committed to dealing with a fish longer and heavier than I at the other end of a line I can break in my two hands, on a rod I can snap across one knee.

Within twenty feet of the bow, the tarpon turns and runs. Another two hundred yards of line vanish. The fish surfaces, shoulders out, and I can hear it breathing, expelling air from the bladder unique to this ancient species, this living Stone Age relic charged with the same primitive forces that powered mastodons and sabre-tooth tigers.

Half-an-hour of runs, first this way, then that, and our meeting assumes a kind of rhythm: the tarpon takes line, I take some back. Often the fish elects to come within twenty or thirty feet, rolls, and without apparent effort, departs, pulling line behind him, almost as if the entire process is a charade. I am acting my part, the fish tells me, but only until it tires of this silliness.

Rain has soaked us now. An hour has gone by. We are the only boat still here, and I wonder what Chick and Jeffrey must be thinking, watching me try to gain an edge, and failing.

I slip on the wet, bow deck.

"You better try to get down into the boat," Jeffrey says. "You could go overboard."

I feel arms around my waist, strong arms. Behind me, in the cockpit, Chick has reached up to hold me, give me support.

A half-century is held in those arms.

Born a year-and-a-half after I was, Chick and I shared the same room for all our childhood, were sent to the same boarding school when I was nine and he was eight, bonded there by the passion of our loneliness, forced by our unspeakable dependence on the other to a kind of compulsive combat, locked in each other's arms in wrestling struggles that would leave our room in chaos, and ended only when the dormitory master, someone, anyone would answer our silent cry, pay us some heed, give us concern, prove that we mattered.

So many embraces in the name of combat, our love's desperate deception. And now this tarpon, this elemental Samson of a fish, has engineered this renewal, this reprise of a fraternal embrace that encloses fifty years.

Twenty minutes more, then another. Chick never lets go. We are closer to the tarpon more often. When it rolls, sighing like a weary steam engine, I can see its huge black eye, as large as a jet tennis ball. The demarcations of the gleaming leaves that are its scales are visible, as are its translucent fins and the awesome nearness of its mystery.

"Be careful, John," Jeffrey tells me. "There is so much strain on that line when it gets this short."

I am too tired to be careful. Indeed, I wonder what further penance will be demanded for my sin of pride, for ever believing I could compete with a such a creature.

He rolls once more, pushes with his tail for yet another run, and the line snaps.

No warning, no time for goodbyes. Snap!

There is no fish, only a gray sea caught in the wind's increasing turmoil and a sky moving quickly to greet the night.

My legs tremble as Chick helps me to the cockpit. He puts a hand on my shoulder. "That was a big fish," he says.

"At least 125 pounds," Jeffrey adds. "Listen, we were going to release him anyway. You almost brought him to the boat."

Of course we would have released him. Yet I also know I wanted to make contact, to run my palm along a line of the armor of his scales, to verify in the consciousness of the fish that we had had this meeting.

Mostly, I am weary, and somehow content because I know that this fish will live as long as I. Each day, each night for the rest of my years I can find this tarpon waiting, held there against the Northwest Channel sky in the purity of that first leap, freed from the sea and linked to me through so much of this stormy afternoon.

"I was beginning to get worried," Ceci says when Chick and I open the gate to the poolside patio. "What were you doing all this time?"

When we tell her, she says, "You mean you stayed out there in this wind and rain with a fish you knew all along you weren't going to keep."

"Have I told you what my father said to me about my fishing?" I ask, and tell the story before she can answer.

"It was after the war, when I was loose, staying out all night, spending the money I'd saved.

"I lived at home, in the family house on East Sixty-fifth Street, where Chick lived when you first met him.

"About six one morning, I opened the front door, still

47

weaving from too much wine, lipstick smeared on my shirt, my dinner jacket a mess.

"My father stood there in the foyer, wearing his bathrobe, directly in front of me, not about to let me pass.

" 'You are not going to use this house as your hotel,' he said. 'Either you get a job this week and start contributing something, or you get out.

" 'I don't know what's wrong with you, John,' he said. 'You can't seem to grow up. You act as if you've never listened to anything your mother and I have been telling you all these years.

" 'I don't know what's going to become of you, John.' He shook his head, his eyes angry, his fists in knots. 'The only two things you care about are fishing and fucking. Nothing else means a damn thing to you.'

" 'Well, you got them in the right order,' I said, and went upstairs to get some sleep.

"Ceci," I say, "after more than forty years, fishing still comes first."

Telling the story, I realize with a tremor that today is my father's birthday—his ninety-sixth. He died twenty-six years ago at the Union League Club in Manhattan, hit with a heart attack as he played bridge late one afternoon. His unfinished martini was left on the table.

Remembering his birthday, I am still in awe of that large man, his determined, unflinching gaze, and the relentless pressures of his demands for excellence. The same heavy, wool bathrobe, made in England for Tripler's, that he wore the morning of our confrontation hangs in my closet. Every now and then, on harsh winter mornings, I wear it to breakfast, thinking about what my father said, seeing him there, his dark eyes blazing with anger at his oldest son's failures.

48

Brunswick

June 17, 1988

According to Henry B. Bigelow and William C. Schroeder, two fisheries biologists and the authors of the seminal work *Fishes of the Gulf of Maine,* a tarpon 5½ feet long was taken off Provincetown, Massachusetts, on July 25, 1915. The authors tell me this is the only record of a tarpon in the Gulf of Maine.

Which does not mean this warmwater fish has not visited more often. Bigelow and Schroeder completed their book in 1925, finishing a project begun in 1912 by the U.S. Bureau of Fisheries, working in cooperation with the Museum of Comparative Zoology of Harvard University and the Woods Hole Oceanographic Institution. Cruising aboard the Bureau's schooner, *Grampus,* from 1912 to 1916, and then aboard the steamers *Albatross* and *Halcyon* after World War I, William W. Welsh was well on his way to completing this first, detailed regional reference when he died suddenly and Bigelow and Schroeder collaborated to finish the work.

For anyone who lives in Maine, as I do, and is interested in fish and fishing, this wonderful book is the irreplacable reference. Given to asides, and unscientific words like "graceful" to describe the Atlantic salmon, it is full of humanity and a great respect for creatures of the sea. Somehow, during the past sixty years, the Federal fisheries establishment has lost its inclination to allow its scientists the human-scale freedom of expression that makes *Fishes* such a delight. Which is one reason why the book has been reprinted many times since its first edition of just 3,500 copies sixty-three years ago.

The quality of its information is another, perhaps more important, reason. In spite of technology's quantum leaps of the past half-century, and in spite of the trillions (whatever a trillion is) of dollars that have flowed through Federal conduits since William Welsh set sail aboard the *Grampus,* woefully little solid research has been directed at comprehending the fishes of the Gulf of Maine, or any other fishes.

In a document produced in 1988 for Conservation International in Washington, author Guido Rahr begins his case for a detailed study of Costa Rica's tarpon with this introduction: "Despite its economic importance, large size (up to 300 pounds) and charismatic qualities, very little scientific research has been done on the tarpon. What has been done has occurred in Florida, site of a major sport fishery. But even there, the details of the tarpon's life history are poorly known."

Having spent the past several days at college and public libraries, and at book shops and other reference centers, I agree with Guido. The major cross-reference I located in several volumes is the weight of the largest tarpon caught on rod and reel: 247 pounds, taken by H. W. Sedgewick on Mexico's Panuco River on March 24, 1938, the day after my father's forty-seventh birthday.

Details of the creature's life—how and where its young are born, its spawning rituals, its migratory patterns, even its growth/age ratios—are uncertain in every case, and admittedly unknown in others. Which might be more understandable if the tarpon were not one of the first fish in America to be classified as a game fish, and one of the most popular and sought-after recreational fish in the angler's lexicon.

With good reason. Tarpon are caught from shore, from bridges, and by anglers wading river deltas and shallow flats. Equipment need not be elaborate, merely sturdy. I can find no record of tarpon taken on hand lines, but I know it has happened, primarily because the fish are partial to a number of basic lures, including such live bait as shrimp, pin fish, and cockroaches. Yes, cockroaches.

I know because several Key West senior citizens (with bottles in their hip pockets, stubble on their cheeks, and precisely the sort of go-to-hell defiance in their bold eyes that I hope will be in mine when I get senior) told me. Watching me cast from the abandoned Navy pier at the Truman Annex, the same pier trod by Harry Truman, Bess, and Margaret as they embarked from the *Williamsburg,* my volunteer advisors suggested I abandon my artificial lures and toss a hooked cockroach to the giant, silver fish lazing in the glow of the pier's lights, rolling twenty feet from me as they turned this way and that in a slow ballet choreographed by the eons of their evolution.

I never had the guts to ask where I might find a cockroach; I did not want to appear more stupid than necessary. If I had been in Key West more than forty-eight hours (which I hadn't) I would not have framed the question, not even in my mind. The island is a sanctuary of giant cockroaches, masters of their fate, captains of their cockroach souls, tough enough to make a meal of your spare tire, big enough to kick a can of Raid from your hand.

These are not the simple characters you might glimpse

51

running from the light in your Bronx kitchen. No journalist, not even Don Marquis, would name these monsters Archy and write poems about them and Mehitabel. Like myself, many Key West new arrivals believe they are stepping away from a land crab when, in fact, the scuttling presence they seek to avoid is one of the island's smaller cockroaches. Put one in the palm of your hand, and your palm is hidden.

How, I have wondered ever since the cockroach bulletin was delivered to me, did the first tarpon ever decide to eat the first Key West cockroach? Perhaps the insect fell to the bay from an overhanging palm where it had been about to drive one of its knees through a coconut husk. Or perhaps it was swept off a pier by a Navy broom, flipped into the Gulf, sucked into a tarpon's chitinous maw, savored like a potato chip, and noted at the memory core of the genetic strand that dictates dietary preference to *Megalops atlanticus,* scientific nomenclature derived from the Greek, meaning "large-headed resident of the ocean edges," which the tarpon surely is.

Only the cockroach whose day ended in the darkness of a tarpon's relatively short digestive tract can verify the primeval circumstances of the fishes' acquired taste. But I can tell you from personal observation that the prophets of the docks, those stubbled scribes who shared their insights, are correct. I have made innumerable casts, most of them failures, with large, brown flies proudly titled Cockroach, and tied specifically to resemble the outsize creatures that stroll the Key West streets hoping some kind soul will toss them a conch fritter.

Flies are not always what they are named, however. Salmon fishermen know the Rusty Rat, an Upsalquitch favorite, has no resemblance to any rodent of any size. Nor would you call in a Silver Doctor for a second opinion. But

in the case of the tarpon fly named Cockroach, the deriva-
tion is direct and instantly identified. It is a mimic of the
living *cucaracha*, and a tarpon will eat it.

Ask Jarrell Andrews, who was eleven years old when
he tested the theory one night at the far end of Key West's
White Street Pier. Before drug dealers desiring darkness
knocked them out of commission, bright lights hung over
the pier's edges, and on the night when cousin Jarrel, his
mother Franny, and father Dwayne strolled with us along
those edges, we could see tarpon gliding in and out of the
light line on the water, fluid silver needles curving from the
dark to the light, then back again, stitching a feeding pattern
among the small fish and shrimp drawn to their doom by
their addiction to artificial illumination.

Dwayne and family had come to visit from Savannah
where Dwayne was born and raised to be unafraid of any
cockroach, no matter how substantial. He threaded one
about the size of a popover onto Jarrell's hook and told the
excited boy (it's difficult for anyone to remain calm watching tarpon in the lights) to toss it over. When he did, Jarrell
stood as alert as any sentry on duty in a combat zone, his
spinning rod held at attention.

Both Dwayne, a fisherman of considerable experience,
and Franny were also equipped to fish, and they cast their
lines into the water. Nothing much happened. Tarpon
swam by, ignoring every presentation, their eyes evidently
on microorganisms we could not see. Franny began talking
about the shops she had toured during the day, and Dwayne
filled in with a notably explicit description of the current
state of his auto radiator sales and repair business, with instructions to Franny that any purchases she might make
would be deducted from her time on this planet.

Through the considerable volume of their dialogue and
over the sweeping sound of seas breaking against the pier's

concrete bulkhead, Jarrell's small, high voice rode in on the wind.

"Hey!" he called. Then, "Hey!" again, louder now. And a third, more drawn out, even louder, "Heeaay! I got something."

He could have said, "Something's got me," and been just as accurate. His small spinning rod was bowed almost double and bucked in Jarrell's thin, clenched hands as line was stripped from the reel. Then the fish departed, the line went slack along with Jarrell, who stared into the darkness, still trying to learn what force from the night had made such violent and unexpected contact.

"What was that?" the boy asked his father.

"One of them tarpon," Dwayne answered without hesitation. "Had to be. Nothing else here could bend a rod like that."

All of us fished harder until midnight, but Jarrell remained the only chosen. The tarpon's mystery survived intact, except for one footnote: the fish do eat cockroaches, a fact Jarrell has noted in his book of life.

I have more empirical evidence of the tarpon's culinary preferences: they also eat crabs. As I watched one evening from the Annex pier, I saw a small crab swimming sidelong, crablike, gently on the water's dark and undulating surface, as soft as velvet under the lights. Then, as if a pressurized boiler taut with trapped air had been cut loose from the bottom, a silver club smote the surface where the crab had been. Crab and fish vanished in a split second, leaving me stunned by the force exerted on behalf of one, small canape.

Crabs, cockroaches, pin fish, silversides, anchovies, water ticks, shrimp, and, I'm certain, other small forms of marine protein feed this imposing fish, giving it the nour-

54

ishment it needs to grow as long as eight feet and as heavy as 350 pounds.

How fast does it grow? The books don't say much. Slowly appears to be the consensus, with a one hundred-pound fish estimated to be somewhere between thirteen and sixteen years old. The species reaches back to the beginning of time: tarpon are the most basic, primitive form of the true bony fishes (superorder *Teleosti*) and they have the primitive looks to prove it, enchanting primitive looks, the kind that would thrill a *Vogue* photographer asked to shoot Brooke Shields alongside a primal presence from the wild.

Large, dark eyes, scales as bright and round as newly minted silver dollars, a vast cavern of a mouth lined with rough, bony plates—armor against all but the sharpest hooks—and a flat, trim torso shaped for swimming speed, these are some of the tarpon features I have noted and the books verify. No one has yet explained why they show up when they do in places they are seen every year. Nor has anyone ever found a tarpon newborn—only larval fry with two weeks or more under their belts have been discovered, wriggling like eels in the shadows of the mangrove roots that protect them.

Peering into the entrails of dead tarpon, caught in nets or by hook-and-line, scientists have discovered females carrying more than twelve-million eggs, which compares to a modern human mother able to double the total population of New York City and Long Island in one delivery at Doctor's Hospital. One thousand tarpon mothers, and that many will navigate the Northwest Channel in one day, can offer twelve-billion newborns to their watery world. An awesome thought, but also an idle one. Until men began killing tarpon at accelerated rates, nature calculated that twelve-million eggs per tarpon mother is just about the right number to keep the species in balance with the entire, vast mosaic of life beneath the seas.

Like many Detroit dwellers eligible for Social Security, tarpon are uncomfortable with temperatures below 75 degrees Fahrenheit. This is why they are year-round residents of southern waters off Mexico, Florida, Costa Rica, Puerto Rico, Haiti, Cuba, Trinidad, Texas, and Alabama, to name a few of the places claiming shores tarpon are known to visit on a fairly regular schedule. The fish have been spotted as far south as Brazil, off northwestern Africa, and on the Pacific side of Central America, which they reach via the Panama Canal. There are, it seems, tarpon in Florida waters year-round, but it is during their spawning season in May and June that they are most in evidence, luring fish watchers like myself to leave wife, home, and gainful employment for a chance to meet these glorious silver beings as they make their dignified passage from beginnings only they can fathom to destinations still a secret.

Able to leap ten feet straight up from the sea's surface, and nearly twenty feet along it, tarpon most often demonstrate this talent when they are hooked. Sometimes, however, they appear to soar just for the fun of it, although scientific observers label the activity "peculiar." I have, I believe, seen tarpon leap higher than ten feet, but that is a story I'm saving. Every now and then, the fish get even with humans on the other end of the line by leaping into, or at, their boats. And, on rare occasions, tarpon jump at people just to say hello. There is a fish in the literature who jumped onto a passing excursion boat, joining a passenger in a deck chair. Another tarpon, so I'm told, broke the neck of a fellow sitting in a skiff in Galveston Bay.

In my opinion, the fish still have a long ways to go to get even. I keep seeing those pale, degrading carcasses in Key West Harbor, and wish leaping tarpon all the luck in the world. Some help, however, may be coming their way. The Florida Legislature has recently enacted a bill to require the tagging of every tarpon killed by an angler. The tags will cost fifty bucks each, and no fisherman may kill more than one fish in a year. Stiff fines are part of the legislation and, as of today, it appears the bill is working. The next step will be the complete prohibition of tarponcide, and any fish brought to a boat will have to be released in good condition.

And, in the tradition of William Welsh and Bigelow and Schroeder, the Florida Keys Fishing Guides Association has located enough grant money to fund a two-year research project to study the life history of the tarpon in south Florida. Dr. John Mark Dean, professor of marine science at the University of South Carolina, will do the work.

Who knows? He may come up with a southern sequel to *Fishes of the Gulf of Maine,* one of my most favorite books.

Robinsonville, NB

June 25, 1974

My clumsiness angers me. If I belonged, if I had been properly introduced to the traditions of Atlantic salmon fishing and the manners of its fishermen, I would be less discomfited. But I have been on the Upsalquitch River just once before, and the humiliation of those two days a year ago still ripples my memory's surface. This morning is on its way to becoming a sequel, and I churn at the prospect of further embarrassment. It will, I know, take a salmon to rescue me, and I am certain I will continue to be baffled by the challenge.

This is, I tell myself, a silly way to fish: standing at the center of a twenty-four-foot wooden canoe, fly rod in hand, casting a trifle of feathers, steel, silk, and thread on the curling current of this remote river, hoping to provoke a salmon's strike. The process requires little skill, I tell myself. After all, Mrs. Hildreth returned to camp last evening with her guide, and he carried a fourteen-pounder she had landed. I have seen her cast and know I can do as well.

But with difficulty. This fly rod, this 9½-foot, slim reed of fiberglass resins and its basic reel with its small handles and schoolboy look, these are not the fishing tools of my saltwater history. These are alien, and demand unfamiliar techniques. I surrender grudgingly, struggling to maintain decorum, as rattled as an actor who forgets his lines on opening night, looking to the wings for escape from public mortification.

And I have an audience. Bill Murray, with all the cockiness of his twenty-one years and his lifetime with this river, is my guide. Or, as he would put it, I am his "sport." The advantage is his. He has brought me here to the river's upper reaches, threading shoals, following channels I cannot see, steering this long, thin canoe with its seven-horsepower outboard, or, when he needs to, paddling or poling with the riverman's steel-tipped pole he himself cut from the forest, peeled, planed, and tipped in perfect replication of other poles made by his father, brothers, uncles, and cousins who share this small, fragile community high in New Brunswick's distant northeast corner.

Two days ago, I drove alone across the 350 miles that separates this forest wilderness from my home in Maine, pondering as I drove the reasons for my return to the site of my prior misery. Pride is one reason. I am certain of that. I think of myself as a fisherman, and a year ago, I left this place with my angling identity woefully unverified.

Joe Sewall, my host, was too gracious to indicate anything but well-mannered concern. "You'll have another chance," he said, after my two clumsy days on the river. "You can try again next year." The farewell of a gentleman, but the words circled ears crimson with my awareness of my shortcomings, and my knowledge that Joe, too, expected I might do better, and was disappointed.

Although we had met once earlier, we got to know each other in Augusta, the state capital, during the 103rd session of the Maine Legislature. Brought together by my work as a journalist and Joe's position as a state senator and chairman of the Appropriations Committee, we learned we shared several friends from earlier days. One of the brightest, most capable, and surely the most charming person then in public office, Senator Sewall was an honest, articulate, and intelligent source of information and insights on the workings of state government, its prospects and its personalities. He could read character in minutes and count House and Senate votes even faster. For a newspaperman like me, just arrived to cover the 103rd, Joe was an invaluable resource who considered it an obligation to keep the public informed. He, his information, and his introductions made my work look good. His friendship and his generosity brightened my life and we became friends.

He kept a fly rod in his office adjoining the Senate chamber, and when I asked him during one lunch hour how anyone could fish with such a long and ungainly stick, he said, "Follow me."

Taking the rod, he went into the deserted Senate, one of the most handsome governmental chambers in New England. Standing in the center aisle, under a soaring domed ceiling trimmed in gilt and corinthian flourishes, Joe stripped twenty or thirty feet from the reel and gave me an indoor casting demonstration. As he lifted his arm and brought hand and wrist straight up and flipped back the large, strong hand holding the rod, the line arced behind him over the high-backed chair on the rostrum reserved for Ken MacLeod, President of the Maine Senate.

When the rod tipped forward, the line followed it, pulling more of itself through the guides. I could hear it whisper as it slid, then fell, almost precisely in the center of the Senate aisle, straight, true, through the doorway leading to the Senate gallery.

"You try it," Joe said after a few more demonstrations.

By then, a dozen spectators had gathered in the gallery, watching with glee, awe, and amazement as the only senator ever to cast a fly in that august chamber held out the rod to a newspaperman, of all people. Uncertain of whether I should even be seen on the Senate floor, much less as a participant in my first fly-casting lesson, I declined.

In mid-June, a few weeks after the incident that kept the State House buzzing for the rest of the session, I found an invitation in the mail. Beneath a silhouette of a leaping salmon engraved on costly paper, the message read: "You are invited to join us at the Upsalquitch Salmon Club for two days of fishing, June 12 and 13, arriving the evening of June 11 and departing after the morning fishing on June 13. RSVP, Joseph Sewall, Robinsonville, New Brunswick, Canada, EOK 1EO."

It took me a while to locate Robinsonville on the map, and several days to inquire about Joe's place. None of the State House lawmakers had been there, but most had heard of it. Joe had bought the lodge and the water two years before, I was told, and had designed and built a new lodge that was one of the finest in New Brunswick. I decided to make the long drive on unfamiliar roads even though that fly rod I'd watched weaving back and forth through the heavy Senate air was the first I'd ever seen in action.

Seven and a half hours after I left home I opened the lodge door in Robinsonville and stepped into a friendly, high-ceilinged room discreetly equipped with handsome creature comforts: a fully stocked bar, glasses engraved with fishing scenes, bookshelves filled with rows of fly-fishing essays, the salmon's life history, and popular novels for those guests who might want to read themselves to sleep. Paintings of fishing moments by Winslow Homer and other artists brightened wood-paneled walls, and recent copies of the *Atlantic Salmon Journal* and other angling publications were arranged in an orderly row along one side of an elegant coffee table. This was, I decided, definitely several cuts above any image of a fishing camp I had conjured as I drove. This was well-planned luxury, and my spirits brightened. I would not, I was relieved to learn, spend my night in a sleeping bag wrestling with mosquitoes and black flies.

Nevertheless, what should have been a gentle rest on a comfortable bed in a private room was disturbed by the swarming of doubts and anxieties that pestered me until dawn. They had begun gathering at supper by the coal stove in the kitchen: a splendid evening meal of thick pea soup, sandwiches on home-baked bread, a lemon-meringue pie with a crust lighter than air. That meal would have sent Hamlet's spirits soaring, but as course followed course, gloom overtook me.

Salmon, I soon learned, and the techniques, times, and places for hooking them, were the only conversational topics that had any chance of survival at that table. The talk was jovial enough, at times boisterous, but it never veered from its focus on the fish that even at that moment, according to Joe, were swimming up the Restigouche and turning the corner at the mouth of the Upsalquitch, on the journey to their upriver spawning grounds that brought them to our doorstep.

For two hours, talk of Rusty Rats, Orange Blossoms, Bogdan reels, Fenwick rods, weight-forward lines, tapered leaders, grilse, taking, not-taking, Home Pool, Mouth Pool, Rock Pool, Mill Brook, Bill Murray, Ollie Moores, Glenn Murray, Jim Moores, Murdock, high water, low water, good water, and bad water rattled off the walls in an endless cascade of salmon-fishing shop talk that seemed specifically designed to underscore my ignorance of the very process I had driven all those miles to experience.

When, with borrowed rod in hand, I stepped into a

canoe at eight that bright morning, I was relieved to learn that I would fish alone with my guide, Glenn Murray. Neither Joe nor his guests would be within watching distance. Only Glenn, who seemed to me young to be a guide, could witness my inaugural day as a fly fisherman.

For almost five hours that morning and again in the late afternoon and evening, I fought the fly rod, the line, the wind, and the impossibly small fly tied at the end of a flimsy, all-but-invisible leader with an affinity for knotting and tangling itself as I waved it around through the air, trying mightily to force the line to straighten, extend itself, and alight on the river's surface with the delicacy needed to avoid traumatizing every fish within a hundred feet of the boat.

I might have succeeded once or twice during the entire day. Each of the rest of my scores of attempts at casting evolved into a melange of small disasters that fired my cheeks with the crimson blush of endless shame. Glenn's day was equally unproductive, but it was irritation that brought blood rushing to his weathered face and kept his temples throbbing beneath the band of his visored guide's cap.

Bent over my leader, frowning at the maze of knots, he somehow maintained patience, tried his best to keep me fishing, changed leaders, changed flies, and, every now and then, offered quiet advice in response to my repeated question, "What am I doing wrong?" "Everything," would have been the correct response, including showing up in Robinsonville with no understanding of even the most fundamental skills required.

By the time the day ended in the long and tender twilight of a northern summer, I was shattered by the weight of my failures. Hour by hour from dawn till dusk, error after error had been added to the tally, until, as I walked the gravel drive from the boathouse to the lodge, I could not rationalize any purpose to my existence in New Brunswick. All that faced me was yet another evening of salmon talk; my potential for participation would be the same at a dinner given by a Serengeti chieftain for his two witch doctors.

I had been on the water for ten hours, and I had seen not one shred of evidence, not one signal, one scale, one turbulent circle on the surface, nothing to indicate salmon, or any other fish for that matter, can live in this crystal river.

Such sterility in fish-bearing waters is not a part of my history. Ever since my early days at Three Mile Harbor, the sea had testified to the presences beneath it. Tails broke the surface, bait fish hissed the desperation of their flight, and often the quarry itself would leap before me, silver scales flashing their verification of life beneath the surface.

But that first day on the Upsalquitch had passed with no such display. I saw only the endless welter of boulders, rocks, and pebbles glaciers had left along the river's winding spine ten thousand years before, each one visible in the light-hearted current, each one rounded smooth by the millenial waters washed over it. I believed I could reach through twelve feet of that water and touch a pebble, such was the river's purity. Surely no fish could hide in the midst of that elemental transparency. Yet even though I had known what to look for, even though I had learned not to doubt my fish-watching skills, I had seen nothing. I could have stared at a glass vase filled with tap water and discovered as much.

Three pairs of eyes searched my visage for clues as I entered the living room to sit by the fire, but I revealed nothing. I struggled to hold the entire day's disaster at the core of my being, knowing that if one tendril of frustration escaped, the entire catastrophe would spill and my humilia-

65

tion would be complete. Not only had I failed to hook a salmon, my fellow fishermen would say, but I had the wretched manners to complain about my misfortune.

When I awoke the next dawn to the soft rumble of rain on the roof above my bed, I smiled for the first time since leaving Maine. That's it for the fishing, I announced to myself. I'll get an early start on the drive home. But when I reached the dining room where breakfast was served us by a cheerful and talented cook, Joe said, "Today's the day, isn't it, John? Get the sun off the water, and the fish won't be so sulky. Nothing they like better than a nice, steady rain."

Not only would fishing continue, I soon understood, but it would have to be pursued with zeal, regardless of the wind-driven rain rattling against the windows like thrown sand. Salmon fishermen, it seemed, simply ignored every element of every configuration.

With breakfast quite finished, departure for the boathouse became my only choice. Looking like a Gloucester deck hand magically transported to Indian country, I soon stood in my canoe dressed in the yellow oilskins of saltwater. My back stayed dry, but the chill rain blew against my face, where it gathered, streamed off my nose and chin down past my clavicle, and from there slid to the inner intimacies of my chest, belly, and loins. And all the while I was expected to cast a fly into the sterile waters of the Upsalquitch as if I actually believed a fish existed there.

If young Glenn Murray acknowledged the weather, he did not do so publicly. From his seat in the stern, his butt in a firsthand meeting with rainwater gathered in the canoe's ribbed insides, he tracked every wavering passage of every cast I made, as if each was on its way toward the maw of a trophy salmon. In the face of his inept passenger, the morning's dismal miseries and the river's apparent poverty, I admired his commitment, even as I questioned the reasons for it.

So when he said, "Look there! Look there!" I not only had no sense of where, but thought he was commenting on the errant sloppiness of my most recent cast, an effort that had put the fly some twenty feet off our stern.

"There he is again," said Glenn, pointing this time.

I followed his arm's line to a circle of the river's surface that bulged, as if a rock just beneath the current forced rushing water to reveal its curving profile. There was, I knew, no rock there. I had been watching the same stretch of water for the past half hour. When the bulge faded as I looked, I knew it had been caused by a living presence.

"That's a heavy fish," young Murray said, still staring at the place on the surface where the bulge had been. "A heavy fish."

"What kind?" I asked. Of each of the uncounted indignities I had inflicted on my guide, that question was the most painful. For once he took his eyes off the river, turned in the stern to look at me, rainwater dripping from his cap's visor, his blue eyes wide, as if he saw some image of ignorance so awesome that it might, indeed, be dangerous.

"A salmon, of course. That there is a big salmon. Maybe twenty-five pounds."

I had seen nothing but the suspect bulge, yet there was in Glenn's taut voice a tremor, the slight trembling of excited anticipation that often betrays even the most seasoned professionals when, at last, they discover the object of their lifelong training and sacrifice.

"Now," he said deliberately, talking more to himself than to me, "now that fish rose twice, but he didn't take.

"Maybe he don't like that fly."

Turning toward me again, his eyes communicating

urgency, he said, "Bring in that line. I'll tie on a different fly. Give the fish a rest."

I turned the handle on the small reel, retrieving the short length of line that had dangled astern. Reaching over the gunwale, Glenn pulled the leader gently through his hands until he reached its end. Putting that in his mouth, he bit through the nylon and picked the unattached fly from the puddle in the canoe's bottom and carefully rested it on the thwart behind him.

Opening a tin fly box, he bent his head close, studying each bit of feathers perched in small rows of colors, like tiny flowers in an aluminum window box. I found his deliberation excruciating. If, indeed, the bulge we had seen was a twenty-five-pound salmon, then I was convinced haste should be the order of the day. Fish I had known tended toward the mercurial, darting here and there, seldom, if ever, holding to one spot long enough for a fisherman to read several pages of angling instructions.

Glenn, however, was quite unperturbed. His motions were the essence of care as he tied on the fly he had selected after reviewing his feathered troops for at least five long minutes.

"Green Butt," he said, "number six hook. The bigger the fish, the smaller the fly. That's what they say, eh?" He held out a black speck no bigger than a button on a baby's shirt. The notion that any creature weighing more than a pound might be deceived or even tempted by such a miniscule offering seemed unrealistic to me, but then, as the past twenty-four hours had taught me, I told myself I had a great deal to learn about whatever it was I was doing at the moment.

"Now," he said, his words each a breath apart, painstakingly enunciated in the twangy accents of New Brunswick Scots, piercing wind and rain with no chance I could misunderstand, "now, begin casting the same way you would if this was the beginning of a new drop, eh? Start close to the boat and work back, about two feet on each new cast. And cast to both sides of the boat, first one side, then the other."

I had learned that much. After six or seven hundred casts, I had memorized the process. Strip off just enough line to make casting possible, flick it off one side at about a sixty-degree angle and let the river's perpetual current carry the fly downstream until it swung straight behind the stern. The only skill I needed to master after I got the cast off was to swing the rod so it followed the fly, keeping the line straight between my rod tip and the lure. Then repeat the process on the opposite side, and then strip two feet more of line off the reel and try again. "Covering the water," I was told, was what I had been doing.

On my fifth cast of the number six Green Butt, as the line straightened behind the stern, a boulder fell from the gray heavens, landed just beside the fly, blowing great gouts of white water into the rainy air.

"Jesus," Glenn said. "He's a heavy fish. Did you prick him?"

I could not answer. Not only did I not understand his question, but when I realized the commotion I witnessed had come from beneath and not from above, I went into shock. Any living thing that could generate that sort of explosion could pose challenges I was not sure I wanted to test. My knees shook.

"Did you prick him?"

"What?"

"Did you feel him on the hook? Did you prick him? Once he feels that hook, he's not coming back."

I began to understand. But I had to try to reconstruct the explosion. I had felt no actual contact through the rod, just my own emotional shock at the sudden eruption. "No, I don't think so. I didn't feel anything."

I stood there in the rain, paralyzed, the line still drifting this way and that in the current behind the canoe. Glenn reached for it and began hauling it in by hand.

"Give him a rest, eh? Have a smoke. Then try him again. He likes the fly, don't he?"

"Seems to," I said, starting to recover, wondering how much further I wanted these developing events to continue.

Glenn took a cigarette from a pack of Players he'd managed to keep dry and lit it with a kitchen match he must have had individually wrapped.

"About halfway into this smoke, and we'll try him again," he said. "Give him a good rest, eh?"

I nodded and sat down, slumping, but never taking my eyes from the spot off the stern where the boulder had fallen.

So this was why we were here. I began to understand. I acknowledged the rain, recognized the reason for my wrinkled, water-soaked fingertips, my saturated underwear, and the chills shuddering along my spine. I had come to hook up with primal force, with a river god.

"Okay," said Glenn. "Try him again."

I stood, and began casting, all but swept away by the anticipation storming within. Those gales subsided with each cast, and when my fly passed the spot where the fish had first charged, I told myself the episode had ended.

"He's gone," I said.

Glenn shook his head, tossing rain drops from his visor. "Keep casting," he said.

By the time my casts reached the limits of my ability, I was convinced the fish had never existed. About fifty feet of line had collapsed in a heap on the river, and I was grateful, as always, when the current tugged at the loops, straightening and correcting my mistakes.

Then, again just as the fly reached the end of its drift, further down stream but close enough for me to look into its open jaws, the salmon appeared, head and shoulders out of water, a wreath of white water around its middle as it rushed the Green Butt.

I yelled, and yanked back on the rod at the moment I felt the fish would engulf the hook.

There was a tap, a split second of resistance that bowed the rod tip an inch or two, and then eternity.

Waiting there for contact to be restored, I knew it wouldn't, and I began wishing I could vanish as totally as the fish.

"You struck too soon," Glenn said. "Took the fly away from him. Pricked him, too."

I needed no such certification of incompetence. The river was there to admonish me. The entire forty-eight hours of my recent past had been destined to define my shortcomings. Even without a witness, I could never again claim to be a fisherman. There was no recipe for my redemption anywhere, no possibility for forgiveness, amnesty, or amnesia. I knew I was cursed to total recall of this day on the Upsalquitch for all the rest of my years.

"It's after noon," Glenn said. "We'd best be heading in." Underscoring the finality of those words with a tug on the anchor line, he freed us from our union with the Upsalquitch and began the short run back to the boathouse.

Yesterday, after a year of bleak flashbacks, I returned to the river of my disaster, and today I continue to hurl myself at its barricades. How many casts have I made? There can be no count. What purpose would it serve to number the

71

times my fly has twitched just beneath the surface, tempting only the stones on the bottom, as if they could break the bonds of density and leap to the sunlight that floods our Upsalquitch.

Perhaps it is the clarity of this day, a flawless blue sky hung over us and the spruce, pine, alder, birch, and poplar that climb the sharp hills shouldering the banks on both sides; or it could be the river's liquid chorus, the lilting melody of falling water that buoys my spirits as easily as it carries a leaf on its journey to the sea. Whatever the elixir of the place, it dispels my gloom.

Helped, I'm certain, by my year-long effort to relieve the paralysis of chronic ignorance. I have spent time in libraries seeking the salmon and have come to know something of *Salmo salar,* this creature of open oceans and narrow streams that has woven its own tapestries of fact and fancy since Caesar's legions watched it leap from streams flowing through ravaged Saxon farms.

More than any other fish of the Atlantic Old World and New, *Salmo salar* has captured Man's fancy. Surely the annual return of the silver creatures—a homecoming announced dramatically at every tumbling waterfall laced with gleaming projectiles shot from the foam by the force of their compulsions—had much to do with early deification. Like the northern sun's December struggle to escape its prison of equinoctial darkness, June's returning salmon reassured agrarian cultures of seasonal renewal and supplied them with some of the finest tasting protein the sea has ever bestowed.

They return to reproduce, these fish. To insure the survival of their species. And this river's headwaters are one of the fast-diminishing spawning and nursery grounds left on the globe. From dark waters off Greenland where they spend their maturing years swimming through a steady rainfall of ocean shrimp, schools of adult salmon begin

72

forming, moving, and finally surging toward their native rivers sometime in late February and early March. By late May, these fish of the Restigouche, Upsalquitch, Miramachi, Kedgewick, Matapedia, and the other salmon waters still singing in New Brunswick and Quebec, are gathered in Chaleur Bay just offshore of Campellton.

As June's long days lengthen, the first, large fish probe the Restigouche delta at Tide Head, their sensors reading trace element combinations locked in some inner, natal memory. So finely tuned are these keys to their heritage that Upsalquitch salmon will swim the Restigouche only as far as the entrance to their home river. Where the rivers meet, the fish will turn and begin the forty-mile journey to the river's headwaters at Upsalquitch Lake.

This morning I wait to meet one them at Noye Pool, a glacial footprint where fast water and depth combine to oxygenate and restore a salmon on its mission of renewal. To reach this place, an Upsalquitch fish has traveled almost a thousand miles, and come six more against the falling waters of its native river.

Like my understanding of the creature, my equipment has improved. My right hand holds no borrowed rod, but the Fenwick 9½-footer given me at Christmas, along with a Pflueger reel and a small, but discriminating, collection of salmon flies: gifts from Jean who purchased them at L. L. Bean after forthright conversation with one of their fishing equipment consultants. It is better outfitting than I deserve; no beginner could ask for more.

It has done little to improve my casting; only practice, and decent instruction, can do that. So I struggle to cover the water, a short stretch at a time, and Bill Murray is ever patient with his sport. I am grateful that yearning is invisible, thankful that the churning of my soul is silent, hopeful that neither Bill, nor Joe, nor the two Hildreth brothers and

73

their pleasant wives can sense the extraordinary dimensions of my anxieties. Landing a salmon, seeing my name in the book of records Joe keeps in such detail, becomes, in this place, an unquenchable flame of competitive desire, searing my insides. If I don't, I tell myself in the warped logic of desperation, I might as well quit.

"Fish rolled there," Bill says evenly, no inflection of excitement, merely a report, like a forecaster saying, "High temperatures in the seventies." Bill has seen fish roll and announced the event a half-dozen times during our two days on the river. I have yet to confirm any such behavior.

"There he is again."

This time Bill points, and I can see the aberrant swirls that a surfacing salmon leaves behind when it moves against the current. They are, I can tell immediately, out of my casting range.

"I don't think I can reach him," I say, hedging what each of us knows is obvious.

"I'll slide back a half-drop," Bill says, reaching for the line that runs the length of the canoe and through the pulley on a bracket at the bow. A submerged lead weight as round and smooth as a cheese is at the rope's far end; its weight holds us, its roundness keeps it from fouling in the rocks. As Bill hauls in line, the weight lifts and we drift backward in the current about thirty feet before Bill releases the rope and waits until our anchor holds.

"There," he says. "You think that's about right, do you?"

I'm not sure what "right" means in this situation, but I know even I can cast far enough to reach the place where the fish was—if, in fact, it is still there.

So I say yes and stand to begin casting. One side, then the other. I cover the water. The fish remains invisible.

74

Bill changes my fly. The Orange Blossom comes off, a Cossaboom goes on.

I cover the water again. I might as well do my casting in a bus terminal.

"We'll give him a rest, eh?" Bill says, reaching for my leader to change the fly again. "Try a Silver Rat this time. That's what that fish took yesterday. Ollie told me."

"That fish," I assume, is the fourteen-pounder Mrs. Hildreth had brought into camp, the very one Joe said we would share at today's luncheon. Visions of the gathering shadow the moment. Can I, I wonder, endure more mannered artifice, more polite salt rubbed in the wounds of my fishless history?

My rod jumps in my hand, as if a tree limb had dropped on the line.

"He's on," Bill says.

I am immobilized. I have done nothing new. This cast is as sloppy as any of the others, yet there is pressure, resistance, a forceful presence at the other end.

There was no warning. Now, what do I do?

The fish decides. After a few long seconds (how many? perhaps three) it moves downstream with a Silver Rat in its mouth. I still hold the rod just as I held it when the fish took the fly. Nothing reacts but my pounding heart.

"Sit down," Bill says.

Sit down? Why sit down? But I do as he says, holding the rod high.

"We'll go ashore." He has already lifted the anchor and, as more line departs my reel, Bill paddles us toward a strip of stones and gravel along the river bank.

"Now," he says when the bow scrapes, "step out and land the fish."

I begin to understand. Feet on the gravel, rod in hand, I

75

am in a situation I recognize: as a surf caster, I have beached striped bass on a rocky shore.

This fish uses the river as its ally, swinging side-to-side in the current, putting strain on the line. Then, just as I want to believe I sense the start of surrender, the salmon soars, leaps clear, suspended silver in the sun, the entire force of its being in stunning profile, its impact on my consciousness as direct as a bullet to the brain.

Luck has joined me. Falling to the river in a rose of white water, the fish has not thrown the hook. This is, I know now, my salmon.

Ten minutes later, Bill's net scythes water where the fish waits, held close by my line. When the net surfaces, the salmon leaps again, but now as prisoner of the mesh around it. Brought to the bank, it is cracked twice on the head by Bill's small club, quivers and dies. Even in the arrogance of my fifty years, even after the desperation of my yearning for verification, I regret my witness of the moment.

But only for the moment.

When we return to the boathouse where the 11½-pound fish is weighed, as I walk the gravel drive to the lodge, I hear the roots of the trees grip the stony ground, feel the river's chill embrace, sense the songs of birds I cannot see, and understand the language of the great slabs of rose granite that line this valley like monuments speaking to me for the first time since I arrived at this brilliant center of the earth.

Arrowsic,
Maine

June 7, 1985

T he Sasanoa River is an
arm of the lower Kennebec, a fork of the primary waterway
and not a river unto itself with its own springs at a distant
source, a course run in solitude and a final embrace by the
sea. Just as a limb branches from a torso, the Sasanoa curves
to the east from the Kennebec, precisely below the Carlton
Day Reed Memorial Bridge that suspends Route One above
Maine's most historic river—the one that carried Benedict
Arnold and his rugged fleet of john boats on their vain invasion of Quebec.

That military presence echoes across the centuries in the
towering cranes of the Bath Iron Works that rise like the
necks of giant, steel herons bent over the river's edge waiting to lift destroyer hull sections from the shipyard floor,
steel shapes that twitch in the morning light, huge minnows
hoisted from their school.

No matter how many times I cruise past the Iron
Works on my way to meetings with the Kennebec's seasonal
abundance of striped bass and bluefish, I can never reconcile

77

the shipyard's blunt industrial profile with the evanescent miracles of plenty this river shelters beneath its placid flow. Once called the northeast's fishiest river by some anonymous statistician who computed the Kennebec's populations of salmon, sturgeon, alewife, herring, striped bass, bluefish, shad, sea-run trout, spearing, flounder, menhaden, eel, white perch, and dozens more major and minor species as the most per cubic yard of any river in the nation, the Kennebec was suffocated by the industrial and municipal wastes of the early twentieth century's profusion of riverside paper mills and the mill towns they spawned.

No fish could breathe in the lower Kennebec; denied its oxygen by vast masses of decaying wood pulp and sulfite wastes from the mills, the river was as lifeless as heavy metal flowing like lava toward a cooling sea. In 1960, shocked by the violence of their neglect, Maine citizens and their legislature put new laws to work to remedy the desecrations of a half-century and the Kennebec clean-up began.

By the start of the seventies, when I drifted this same Sasanoa in a slab-sided Banks dory, the first schools of striped bass had returned, dappling salt marsh coves with their tentative feeding forays. And today, more than a decade later, we are all but certain that we shall meet school bass here in this quiet water.

There are three of us aboard Brad Burns' twenty-three-foot Aqua-Sport: Brad, myself, and a first-time fisherman. This is perhaps the 125th dawn I have fished with Brad from the *Sea Beagle;* the first was several years ago and it followed a phone call from Brad after he'd read a fishing column of mine.

"I know the Kennebec," he told me, with no qualification and much robust assurance. "I've fished that river most of my life and I can almost guarantee you a striper over forty pounds."

That promise, kept many times, was the start of a relationship built on our mutual love of fishing, striped bass, the Kennebec, and Maine. A generation younger than I, but older in many ways, Brad is the grandson of a Maine lobsterman and the son of an Iron Works welder. He snarls at the high cranes each time we pass them on our way to another world. He curses the price his father paid in body and spirit in the name of regular wages and an easement from the mortal demands exacted by year-round lobstering in the Gulf of Maine.

Brad returned to the sea his grandfather lived by, but on different terms. As independent as his ancestral lobsterman, Brad began selling office equipment as soon as he graduated from college. In less than a year, he started his own company, got a copy machine franchise from Toshiba just as office copiers became essential equipment for even the smallest business and Portland's economic boom took flight on the wings of newly arrived squads of bankers, attorneys, brokers, engineers, and their platoons of service support groups. Before he was thirty, Brad was making more money than his father and grandfather had ever imagined a Maine working man could accumulate in their economically undernourished state.

But six-figure incomes had no effect on his Yankee traits or his maritime heritage. Brad bargained the Aqua-Sport dealer to dust when he bought his boat, and he makes many of his own rods and lures. What he cannot make, he buys wholesale in vast quantities. His occupation and his fishing mania combine with the tug of his Yankee genes to create a fast-moving contradiction. If his personna dressed to its identity, Brad would be wearing a three-piece business suit with hip boots and a sou'wester. And he'd be carrying a fishing rod in one hand and a Toshiba sales order in another.

His determination to be best, his awesome commitment to competition, is the reason for both his business success and his mastery of the Kennebec. He is not about to be beaten out of a Portland sale nor is he going to allow a single striped bass to elude him. This combination of the innate comprehension of the sea and its marine surroundings that Brad inherited and his compulsive need for success make him one of the most knowledgeable and productive striped bass hunters on the Kennebec.

My own competitive gears have slipped a bit with age, and I am too much a romanticist ever to invest as much energy and electronic equipment as Brad has in trying to locate the home address of every striper in the river. In that sense, we are quite different, and I often wondered why he phoned in the first place, and have been even more confounded by his generous willingness over the many years to take me along on so many of his fishing trips. But as those adventures unfolded and as I visited his Falmouth home more frequently, I began to understand. Brad's mother is a painter, an artist whose landscapes and still lifes are hung in each of the rooms in that comfortable, but Yankee, house. The gentle sensitivity of those paintings is also part of Brad, and it surfaces from time to time. He senses from reading what I write that I love striped bass, and it is that he relates to.

Because he too loves the fish. During my years on the *Sea Beagle,* he and I must have hooked and landed more than five hundred stripers, many of them more than thirty-five pounds. None of those fish, to the best of my observations, has died. The entire operation aboard Brad's boat is designed with hook-and-release fishing in mind. Every hook is barbless, tackle is sturdy enough to land fish in the minimum time. Often Brad shouts at me to pay attention to my work, to put more effort into my end of the fight with a big bass. Once aboard, each fish is unhooked as painlessly as possible, laid flat on the transom with a wet towel over its head to keep it motionless, measured, tagged, weighed, and slipped back to the river from Brad's firm hands. Every so often, the ritual is accented by a kiss. If the emerald mosaic of the striper's markings gleams especially bright along its back, or the dawn seems to fly more than a mere day from its eastern banners, Brad raises the fish to his lips and gives it a full-fledged buss before he sets it free.

Often when he does, he turns to see if I'm watching. When his eye catches mine, he blushes and flashes a schoolboy grin—a schoolboy caught with a bunch of crumpled violets picked for the girl in the front row. In his own mind's eye, and as he hopes his copy machine competitors see him, Brad is the contemporary Maine executive, as ruthless as any Wall Street vice president. The emotional intensity of a spontaneous kiss reveals too much humanity to sustain that image and Brad is always more awkward with the self-revelation than I.

His obsession with the striped bass is his acknowledgment, conscious or otherwise, of his maritime heritage. In some ways, I'm sure, he is ill at ease with his suits and his organizational behavior. His grandfather's nobility beckons from every lobsterboat we pass. His father's craftmanship and drudgery slide down the Iron Works ways whenever a new destroyer is launched. But no sails flap on a copy machine, no waves break over the bow of Brad's Mercedes. Through his courtship of the striped bass, he makes amends for being the first of the Burns men to abandon a life of ships and the sea.

The striper benefits from the affair. Other fish are granted no exceptions. Like most Maine-coast Yankees, Brad looks to the Atlantic for sustenance. Several days each season, he and the *Sea Beagle* head twenty miles offshore

81

with a bucket of surf clams on deck, clams salvaged from the Higgins Beach waterline after great swells of a storm at sea wrenched them from their homes beneath the sand and hurled them naked from the surf for Brad to harvest, freeze, and use as bait. Just as Wyman Aldrich slashed open his skimmers with a stiff, sharp knife, Brad gets his hands wet with hen-clam gooslum as he weaves sloppy chunks of meat onto codfish hooks that do their silent work some fifteen fathoms down.

As the *Beagle* heaves on the endlessly restless waters of the Gulf of Maine, Brad hauls handlines and spends a day filling the boat's fish boxes with mottled sea-brown cod, a few hake, and every once-a-year or so, a halibut: the food-fish prize of these waters. On the long trip home, herring gulls and great blackbacks stream behind the *Beagle* like white pennants trailing as Brad heads and guts his catch, transforming his day's work to freezer-ready slabs of fresh-caught protein. It's on those cold voyages that memories of his father and grandfather come aboard.

I am always invited, but always demur. Cod are not a favorite of mine, neither on a line nor dinner plate. And there is something more, although neither of us has talked it out. I have a feeling Brad will become someone else if I meet him on another stage. On the Kennebec and its approaches with striped bass as our only priority (although we will accept a bluefish if it comes our way) we each know where the other stands. We share our mutual affection for this creature and let our other considerable dissimilarities slip away as easily as the bubbles in our wake.

Our trips are rituals certified by time. I drive in darkness to an all-night eatery, often as early as three-thirty so we will be certain to be on the river before June's quick dawns. We are so early we overlap with others who are ending their long evenings instead of beginning a new day.

High-school seniors, weary from their proms, their beers, pot, and back-seat fumbles bend their lipstick-smeared faces over steaming cups of black coffee, blanching as they watch Brad and me devour eggs-over-easy, bacon, and soggy slabs of butter-drenched toast.

Brad is a large man and a big eater. His half-bald head came early in his busy, worried thirty-seven years, and the fringes of gray hairs rise from a big-boned frame that supports a fairly rotund 220 pounds. His features too are rounded; there has been too much good living, too few days hauling lobster traps. But above the apple cheeks are the cold, blue eyes, the water-blue eyes, the sharp all-seeing blue eyes that Yankees give their sons and daughters century after century, generation after generation. If I could carve seventy-five pounds of fat from Brad (and I could) I would reveal Captain John Smith, or, more likely, his third mate, recruited in some Bournemouth tavern where he drank up most of his wages as a deck hand aboard a coasting schooner, appraising every seafarer who came through the door with the same blue-eyed, hard-eyed stare Brad gives the ersatz Hell's Angel who bulls by our booth as we mop our plates with toast.

It is still dark when we reach the river. Not even a gleam violates the black horizon in the east. I help unload gear from Brad's four-wheel-drive pick-up and carry rods, reels, and lures to the pram. When Brad eases onto the single center thwart, his mass cuts our freeboard to less than two inches. I have to hang my ass over the transom to give the little boat a semblance of trim. A jet river slips by, always turbulent here, caught between the tides from the sea and the downstream tumble of five other rivers that join the Kennebec in Merrymeeting Bay, a dozen miles upstream. It is this blending that generates the river's remarkable abundance. The shoal Merrymeeting with its vast flats of marsh grasses and wild rice spawns limitless legions of diatoms and microbes that are the essential nourishment of the larval infants that will grow to become tiny fish, the next link in the river's rich food chain.

Here where the *Sea Beagle* is moored one hundred yards offshore, fresh water and salt water meet in a roiling, brackish confusion of currents and counter-currents that can disconcert small fish and make them easier meals for striped bass holding effortlessly in eddies, waiting for the river to tumble breakfast their way. Always the first to step aboard, Brad clambers over the *Beagle*'s rail as the pram, relieved of his bulk, rises like a bubble from below. I hand gear over the gunwales, then climb aboard as Brad lifts a hatch, turns a fuel-line switch, closes the hatch, and starts the engine.

We are off, headed downriver on an itinerary etched over the years in Brad's daily logs that record where, when, and how every striper has been discovered. Depending upon the month, the week, the day, the time of the tides, the wind and the weather, we will fish Goat Island, Bailey Cove, Pond Island, Bald Head, Popham Beach, the Morse River or any of the other scores of bass-gathering grounds marked on the charts of Brad's memory. I never know where we will be fishing until we arrive.

In the silence forced by the engine's roar, watching our wake as the lights of the Iron Works wink and disappear, a thousand dawns beckon from the darkness. From Gardiner's Bay to Montauk, from the first striped bass I hauled ashore on East Hampton's Georgica Beach, the fish has been my talisman. From the Manhattan I left and the Long Island that lives in my memory, the fish has stayed with me, waited for me in the Maine that is now my home and welcomes me to this river. Brad and the *Sea Beagle* allow me to respond to that welcome, and for this I am forever grateful. Thirty-five years link these Kennebec stripers with that first, sand-covered fish I held in my arms as the sun touched the Georgica dunes. Thirty-five years and my heart still races as tentative light buds in the east and I know that once again my life's icon will soon roll somewhere on this river's satin surface to reassure me of nature's sustaining continuity.

For more than a year now, prodded by Brad's stubborn commitment, he and I have worked together to accelerate that natural process. Once home to a native, spawning, year-round striper population, a renewed Kennebec, so Brad's reasoning goes, may respond well to efforts to regenerate that resource. Our plan is simple: import striper fingerlings from hatcheries along the Hudson or Chesapeake, release them in Merrymeeting's friendly habitat and hope they survive three Maine winters in the Kennebec's deepest reaches and then, in their youthful maturity, successfully spawn and hatch a native brood, true Kennebec stripers like those netted by the barrelful from beneath thick January ice at Winnegance almost a century ago.

We see the effort as a way to repay the fish and the river for all the mornings they have bestowed. Brad works mostly at operations and personnel; his sales energies are right for the job of taking on Maine's Department of Marine Resources and for locating first-rate fingerlings and getting schedule commitments. I am the fund-raiser, and Brad has set a budget of some $2,500 for this, our second year. Last September, we released 1,000 three-inch stripers; before this fall arrives, we hope to have more than 10,000 lined up and paid for. Marine Resources is enthusiastic about the effort and will provide the special tank trucks needed to bring the fish safely from a federal hatchery in South Attleboro, Massachusetts.

I write letters to a few friends, men and women who either love fishing, especially the striped bass, and others who have enough money to be able to give The Kennebec

River Striped Bass Restoration Fund a hundred, painless, tax-deductible bucks. One of those letters goes to a young man named Pritam Singh, a Portland and Boston real-estate developer, a contemporary and classmate of our own sons who has become wealthy early in what has been at best a turbulent life. I have known him since his stormy high-school career in Brunswick swirled him into my life. He has asked several times to come fishing with me and when he gets the Restoration Fund letter he sends a check for $1,000: more money by far than we ever hoped to get from any one donor. Along with the check there is note about his enthusiasm for the project and a wish that he might see the Kennebec and its stripers first-hand.

Brad knows a good thing when he sees a one-thousand-dollar check and he tells me to invite Pritam to come along anytime. Today is the day, and Pritam stands beside me, the third man on deck and one of the few first-time fishermen ever to come aboard the *Sea Beagle*.

And quite probably the only turbanned fisherman ever to wet a line in the Sasanoa in the river's long history. Pritam is a Sikh by choice, and Sikhs are bound by their dogma to wear their turbans whenever they rise from their beds, no matter what the day's activities might be. When I relayed Pritam's request to come fishing, Brad's first question was, "Do you suppose he'll wear that turban?"

The incredulity and disapproval in his tone mirrors the entire Portland business community's reaction to Pritam and his costume. Maine's largest city is still a Yankee town; moderation, restraint, and conformity are behavioral standards for Cumberland Club members and the men and women (a few) who meet for lunch in private dining rooms atop the high-rise banks that sprout each year from cobbled streets. There are very few indeed among these suited and

86

briefcased legions of the city's factotums who are unaware of Pritam Singh and his turban.

Pritam is nourished by the attention. It is his sustenance, his sun. Too long ignored as a child, shunted from one home to another, one neighborhood to the next, from Seattle, Washington, to Brunswick, Maine, his shaky identity sustained only by the force of his own bitterness, he has, in a remarkable demonstration of grit and ego, built his own unmistakable persona with his turban as its most visible hallmark.

Born Paul LaBombard in Fitchburg, Massachusetts, some thirty-three years ago, he was raised by a mother who bore him at seventeen, a year after she had gone to work in the same Fitchburg textile mill where her mother had begun working when she was sixteen. Paul's mother, Rose, and his namesake father, both second-generation French-Canadians and devout Catholics, had a convulsive relationship that included three divorces and three re-marriages. There was never enough money for the four LaBombard children, nor was there always a home. Young Paul was sent to live with "aunts" so many times the home concept never materialized for him as a child, and troubles him still as he moves from one building to another, one city to the next.

He has the wherewithal to move wherever he pleases. This, too, is a creation of his need. Nine years old, in the front row of a dusty Fitchburg elementary school third-grade class, Paul LaBombard stood and answered his teacher's question about what he would do as a grown man. "I will never be poor," said the pale boy with pale, azure eyes, staring relentlessly in near-sighted concentration, his face stiff with rage and determination. "I will never be poor."

He had yet to keep that pledge when he first came to

our home some seventeen years ago. A high-school junior whose father had been transferred to the Brunswick Naval Air Station where he served as an ordinary seaman, Paul LaBombard found friends among our sons, their friends, and the several adolescent boys who seemed to be forever at our house, eating the dinners Jean cooked, sometimes for a dozen hungry teenagers. Those were restless times, the late sixties, times of psychedelic bullshit, drugs, and over-amplified music as well as times of torment in Southeast Asia, Memphis, Los Angeles, and the streets of Dallas.

LaBombard, as we called him then, found a market of sorts for his first entrepreneurial efforts when he and our foster-son Roger began baking banana skins in Jean's oven, shredding the results and selling the mystery substance to less intelligent fellow students who believed Paul and Roger when they promised an "incredible high" to smokers of the stuff that had come straight from a supermarket produce counter, wearing its original Chiquita labels.

From bananas, the Paul/Roger team moved on to oreg-ano, also smoked in joints rolled with E-Z Wider cigarette papers, just like the ones carried by every hard-rock musi-cian worth his claim to hip. Like a great many kids in those times when the entire American value system had been un-dermined by leaders who lied, Paul and Roger lived in a kind of illegal limbo: they never pressed their luck hard enough to be labeled outlaws, but if that luck had deserted them, they would have had some tough explaining to do. Paul tried, but he never found wealth in high school.

Fate and his slowness afoot set other events in motion, however, which started him down the road to riches. In the spring of 1970, Paul and Roger joined tens of thousands of other young Americans in front of the Washington Monu-ment, where they raised their banners of protest against the Nixon Administration and its policies in Southeast Asia.

Arrowsic, Maine ✦ *June 7, 1985*

When Attorney General John Mitchell's gas-masked militia began dispersing the protestors, billy clubs were swung, thousands of heads were bloodied, and more thousands of prisoners were taken. Chased by a posse of National Guardsmen, Roger ran faster than he ever had during the touch-football games on our lawn, and he escaped. Paul, who watched those games and seldom ran for any reason, did not.

For three days and long nights, he and his fellow detainees waited anonymously in the basement chamber of a Department of Justice building. Their diversions included throwing peanut butter sandwiches against the ceiling and taking bets on how much time would pass before they dropped. Paul played the prisoner's game, but he also stared at the Capitol dome through barred windows and pondered the shattering of any previous allegiance he had pledged his government. Just as his parents had sentenced him to other, anonymous homes, so, it seemed to him, the very government he had been taught to respect had proven itself unworthy of trust.

For this son of French-Canadian parents and a product of their unshakable Catholic faith, the loss of his civic institutions combined with the denial of his childhood needs proved shattering. With next to nothing to sustain his soul, Paul LaBombard left that Justice Department holding tank, took a last look at the Capitol and headed south, away from his home in Maine, away from his Fitchburg memories, away from the few friends he had in Brunswick, and toward whatever lonely independence he might find when he reached Key West, the last and southernmost stop on U.S. Route One.

In July he traveled north, this time to a farm in Nova Scotia worked by two women he met in Key West. From there, in the fall, he moved to Amherst, Massachusetts, a town of five campuses, a place where attending classes without enrolling was not only possible but a way of educational life for a good many young disciples of the Age of Aquarius. It was in one of those purloined classrooms that Paul LaBombard heard of the farm in nearby Montague that would change his life forever.

By the time Paul knocked on the farm door, the large, rambling building that had once been a two-hundred-acre truck farm had become a spiritual commune under the leadership of Guru Shabad, formerly Stephen Josephs, son of well-to-do parents who had contributed significantly to the farm's purchase and its maintenance. No one who agreed to abide by the rules was turned away and Paul LaBombard was not one to quibble when it came to finding a bed and three vegetarian meals a day.

During the winter of 1970-71, the commune's religious ties to those of Yogi Bajhan were significantly strengthened. From his headquarters in Santa Fe, the Yogi operated an increasingly effective effort at recruiting young, middle-class Americans as new converts to Sikhism. Guru Shabad converted and led each of the others at Montague through the dogmas and rituals of the Sikhs, an Indian sect with world headquarters at the Golden Temple in Amritsar in the mountains of Punjab.

As his fellow Montague farmers chanted, Paul LaBombard became Pritam Singh. A few months later, he married a former Smith College senior now named Gruden, and a few months after that stood by her bedside as their daughter was born. The man who had come to Amherst with no faith and no family now had both.

Seeking still more reassurance, he left Montague the following year with his wife and infant daughter on a 6,000-mile journey to the Golden Temple where he stayed for several months. Fully committed to the Indian Sikhs and their faith, he returned to Portland and with a portion of her inheritance, he and Gruden opened Pritam's first real entrepreneurial enterprise: a toy store on one of Portland's boutique streets. The shop was named Child's Play and Pritam hired his old friend Roger as his sole salesperson, bookkeeper, and manager. The ties between Pritam and our family were re-established.

From Child's Play, Pritam moved on to several other retail ventures and then discovered the fast-track world of urban real estate. Bright enough to analyze the benefits of federal and state tax incentives to encourage the rehabilitation of historic structures, Pritam borrowed at low interest and sold his improved properties for large profits, a formula that made him a small fortune just as it did for scores of other real-estate high rollers in those days of Portland's boom.

It's been almost ten years since Child's Play, and the bearded, turbanned man standing on the *Sea Beagle*'s deck with a spinning rod held awkwardly in his hands has solidified his image, and his bankroll for all I know, as a young millionaire. The patterns of circumstance, fate, and magic that led him from our kitchen table in the sixties to a berth alongside me on the *Sea Beagle* in the eighties are woven in a tapestry of events so disparate and so remarkable that no one but myself could believe or comprehend them. The mere fact that Pritam, in "that damn turban," is aboard Brad Burns' boat is as unlikely as finding a gold nugget floating in a Kennebec eddy.

It is fishing that has waved the wand. Fishing has put a nonconformist former French-Canadian waif aboard a boat owned by a Yankee conformist of the old school, and it is fishing that has put me between them, made me the one that brought together this odd couple and energized a further series of events that will introduce more fish to more unlikely fishermen in more exotic places than most anglers can expect from several lifetimes. On that contentious morning in Manhattan, I should have told my father just how far fishing would take me. But then, how was I to know?

How appropriate that my adventures should begin with one, exquisite four-pound striped bass.

And one that arrives when it's needed most. Because the picking on the Sasanoa this morning has been slow, a mere iota from motionless. If it were not for Pritam and my eagerness to have him hook his first striper, I would be content simply to be here in this wide section of the river dotted with hummocks of marsh grass and with small islands strewn with granite boulders left in agreeable jumbles by a glacier 10,000 years ago.

There are places on the Sasanoa that a milennium has not changed. The same ledge juts from under the roots of scrub oak, pine, and bayberry—pink granite unmarred by man, smoothed by the river ice of 10,000 winters, scrubbed by the floods of 10,000 springs. Even though I know Iron Works cranes rise less than a half-mile from our drift, I am in closer touch with the primeval, with river, marsh, sky, and shore just as they have always been.

And on this late spring morning, Maine's shy blooming has begun. Reluctant oaks are greening at last, the emerald of their awakening bright against the darker pines and spruce. Marshes dun and stooped by the last ice of March are revived, their green even more delicate than the budding oaks. Under a sun now surging toward the zenith of its northern arc, life soars. The shortness of northern summers grants us this intensity, breaks our hearts with beauty even as autumn's acorns are born and terns race to breed before they must cross the equator once again.

This shallow river is warming. As the tide falls, mud

flats' black shoulders soak like great lizards in the sun, gulping heat to be stored for rising waters when the tide turns. It is this warmth that releases small shrimp from their winter immobility, shrimp in such countless numbers their random spasms are a downpour on the Sasanoa's quiet surface. These shrimp bring the stripers here on these June mornings. In two weeks, another drama will open on another river stage and we will fish another place where other logics prevail.

But today, if there are striped bass in the Sasanoa, they will most likely be here. They would be, surely, if they understood the importance of their meeting with Pritam.

He has not said as much but his expression tells me he is beginning to change his opinion of Brad as a fish finder, and his opinion of my claims that Brad is the best there is.

Still, Pritam keeps casting with one of Brad's light spinning rods, dutifully reeling in the small Rebel lure, this one wearing a single set of barbless treble hooks. His casting is stiff; like so many beginners, Pritam has not learned how to let the rod's built-in tensions and resilience do the work. But he gets the lure out there with sheer effort, and it drops on still, gray water unmarked by any signal of feeding fish. Blind casting from a drifting *Sea Beagle* turning slowly in the current is not Brad's idea of the best way to spend a fishing morning. But his charts and instruments and years of early-season bassing tell him unequivocally that he is in the best of all possible hunting grounds. So Brad grits his teeth and here we stay.

The ebbing tide nudges us toward the Sasanoa's narrowing, a stretch where advancing marshes pinch the broad upper water, shape it for the coming tumble of Hell's Gate, the river's stormiest passage through a granite chasm that has awed navigators for centuries.

Brad leaves off his casting, heads for the controls, ready

to start the *Beagle*'s engine and power us upriver for yet another drift. Just as Brad's large hand nudges the starter button, Pritam yells.

"I've got one!"

And he does. Fifty feet off the *Beagle*'s stern quarter a broad tail swipes white water across the surface, then vanishes as line strips from Pritam's untended reel.

"Try not to reel while he's stripping line," Brad says, his tone skating the edge of the impatience instructors have for slow learners. Pritam pays no attention. He has found the reel handle and turns it relentlessly.

Studying the rod's curve, I can tell the fish is not a slammer, not some fifteen or twenty-pounder who can cause trouble on the light rig. I reach through Pritam's busy hands and tighten the drag just a bit. With the current accelerating as the fish nears the lower river's fast water, Pritam needs the advantage.

He is swept away by the excitement but trying to appear properly collected. Above all, he does not want to lose this fish. That is one conclusion to the encounter that could cast doubt on his competence, doubts his shaky self-esteem as a fisherman does not need.

Both Brad and I want the fish to hold, to see it on the transom, gleaming with the brightness of its vitality in the luminous June sun. And we want to share Pritam's exultation, the joyous rush that fishermen know when they can touch the slick scales and read the braille of a wild creature's essential mystery.

"Keep him coming," Brad says as Pritam pauses, stops reeling and watches the striped bass, visible now, fifteen feet behind the stern, its brilliance flashing beneath the pale water.

Grunting as he feels resistance, Pritam reels and lifts his

rod tip in response to my repeated instruction, "Keep that tip up."

Bending his bulk across the stern, Brad reaches for the leader, grabs it, sees that the fish is well hooked, and hoists it aboard with one fast sweep of his arm. Once the striper is in the cockpit, Brad lowers it to the deck, quickly extracts the barbless hooks, and lays the fish on the transom.

"Nice fish," he says. "Aren't they beautiful?"

"How much does it weigh?" asks Pritam, his blue eyes dancing, his smile wide.

"About four pounds. A nice fish," Brad says.

Pritam reaches and touches the fish. Brad looks at me, then back to Pritam. The fish should be released.

"It's my first striper," Pritam says. "The first one of my life." He knows what is expected aboard the *Sea Beagle*. "Can't we make an exception?"

"Your first fish," Brad says. "Sure, why not."

The striper is slipped into the fish well, not the Kennebec. Pritam holds the well cover open, looking at the fish for a minute or more. He takes a deep breath, turns to me.

"That was fun," he says. "I like fishing." He pauses, lowers the cover on the fish well, looks directly at me with those intense eyes. "Where," he asks, "is the best fishing in the world? What kind of fish?"

I wanted to say, "Right here on the Kennebec," but I knew he would not understand. We had been drifting and casting for almost three hours and he had one four-pound reward for what he considered an inordinate amount of time and effort.

"That depends," I answer. "If you are after size alone, you ought to try the waters off New Zealand or Capo Blanco. Get some of those 1,000-pound marlin, like Zane Grey and Hemingway.

95

"But that's fairly exotic," I say, catching Pritam's frown. "Plenty of people in Maine will tell you the Atlantic salmon is the most exciting fish that swims."

"Where can you catch those?" Pritam wants to know.

Again, I could say the Kennebec, or the Sheepscot, or the Narraguagus, or the Penobscot, all here in Maine, but I know Pritam wants adventure and fish, and catching a wild Atlantic salmon in any of Maine's rivers is an achievement of patience as well as skill, and Pritam has less patience than skill, even though this is his first fishing day.

"Probably New Brunswick and Quebec," I explain. "You might still be able to get a few days at one of the fishing camps."

"Is that the best there is?"

Pritam won't quit, so I keep talking. "Well, some people will tell you Iceland is better for Atlantic salmon. The fish are generally smaller, but there are more of them. At least, that's what I've been told."

"Who told you?"

"Bob Manning," I answer, sensing now that this grilling will end with a decision of sorts. "I worked in his building when I lived that year in Boston. He spent a week that summer in Iceland and we talked about the fishing there."

Pritam has made a decision. "Let's go to Iceland," he says, his smile back and broad.

"This summer?"

"Yes, this summer. Can you reach Manning and get the details? Find out how we get there, where we stay, how we fish. Find out if the fishing is really good."

"I think Manning is still in Boston. A trip to Iceland is expensive," I add. "Probably two or three thousand dollars a person for a week, at least, plus the cost of getting there."

"Want to come along, Brad?" Pritam asks, and I realize that the scope of the cost makes a fishing trip to Iceland precisely the sort of notch he wants to cut to verify the dimensions of his entrepreneurial success.

Brad's look questions me. I'm not sure if Pritam is serious. Or, if he is at this moment, whether he will be tomorrow. I have lived through many of his impulsive moments and have learned that he can change his mind easily and often. "I'll call Bob Manning," I reply, "and I'll get back to you."

Pritam walks to the stern, standing there in his navy-blue turban and white tunic as we turn the bend and Brad steers the *Sea Beagle* under the bridge and into the Kennebec. As we cruise past the Bath Iron Works under a bright midday sun, Pritam lifts the well cover for another look at his prize.

"Beautiful, isn't it?" he says, grinning.

Yarmouth, Maine

August 30, 1987

Asummer Sunday morning in Gertrude McCue's kitchen in her handsome Yankee home on a street where other Euclidean mansions parade in their white, clapboard dress uniforms—New England's frontline troops protecting a fine past from an advancing present. Gertrude has taken us in, Jean and I. We arrived like waifs from Key West two months ago, forced north by one of my impulsive and intemperate decisions. Our home in Brunswick is rented and will be until the year's end.

The gentility of Gertrude's kindness humbles me. My failure as an engineer of my finances and career nettles, stinging a bit more each day. But the glories of this house, the monuments to grace that stand here on foundations two centuries strong, these pleasure me with their testimony to the rightness of proper Bostonians and their gentle manners.

This morning, as plump maple leaves flutter in an early breeze and roses strain themselves to bloom on this exemplary midsummer day, I am reading about myself and Brad and striped bass in the *Maine Sunday Telegram* and I am feeling better than I have in months. How artfully this creature keeps weaving itself through the confused fabric of my life. If, as I have claimed, I was not once a striper, then surely the fish must once have been I.

"John Cole of Brunswick," writes Paul Carrier in the *Telegram,* "a longtime devotee of the striped bass, was so excited by the recent discovery of twenty-six newborn stripers in a Merrymeeting Bay estuary that he gleefully proclaimed it, '. . . the best news of the century . . .'

"That may overstate the case a bit, but state officials, anglers and conservationists clearly are delighted by the find, which marks the return of a troubled native species once so plentiful in the region that nineteenth-century fishermen netted thousands at a time.

"The birth of newly hatched bass in the Eastern River is a unique success story, according to the state Department of Marine Resources, because it is believed to be the first self-sustaining restocking of striped bass in New England coastal waters.

"The numbers are small—twenty-four fish from one location and two others found elsewhere in the estuary—but state officials say the capture of more than two dozen young stripers during routine fish population tests signals the presence of many more.

"By reintroducing the bass here, enthusiasts say, Maine may set an example for other states as conservationists try to revive a species that has been in decline for decades. That, in turn, will offer yet another reminder that environmental damage can be undone, particularly when fouled rivers are allowed to cleanse themselves.

"'This documents that they can successfully reproduce themselves there,' said Don Kimball of the U.S. Fish and Wildlife Service, which cared for some of the fish until they were old enough for stocking. 'Now it's just a matter of building up the numbers.'

100

Yarmouth, Maine ✦ *August 30, 1987*

"The striper is in trouble all along the eastern seaboard, a victim of forces that may include overfishing, water pollution, and acid rain. The situation is particularly desperate in Chesapeake Bay which produces up to 90 percent of the East's migratory striped bass.

"State records indicate that bass ascended the Kennebec as far as Waterville in the nineteenth century, and spawning occurred in both the Kennebec and the Androscoggin at that time. But the construction of dams to develop water power blocked traditional spawning grounds upriver, and the growth of Maine's paper mills sealed the fate of the stripers by polluting the rivers.

"Hoping for something more than seasonal visits from migratory bass, Cole and Brad Burns of Falmouth and others set out to create a native population in the Kennebec and Lower Androscoggin, thereby re-establishing the stocks that lived year-round until the fish disappeared by the 1930s.

"The project began on a small scale and grew slowly until 1985 when more than 46,000 Hudson River fingerlings purchased from a hatchery in New York were transferred to the Kennebec. Last year another 31,000 were released in the Kennebec and the Androscoggin.

"'We just wanted to see the native run of fish restored as it deserves to be,' said Burns. 'We are going to face the day, in short order, when we are going to have to enjoy this creature more for its beauty than for what we can do with it in a frying pan,' he said."

As the sun spills over my toast, coffee, and *Sunday Telegram,* I think: 46,000 fish in 1985. That's the year Pritam caught his fish on the Sasanoa.

How much would have happened differently if that striper had decided it wasn't hungry.

101

Laxa Y Leirasveit, Iceland

August 15, 1985

Howard Clifford is across the Home Pool from me, quite dry even though he wears chest waders, standing at the very edge of a rock just below the waterfall that cascades white into the river at his feet. He is making short casts with a light fly rod, dropping his wet fly, a Green Butt, I believe, into the confused water at the base of the falls and letting it drift downstream on a brief, turbulent journey. It is almost four in the afternoon and we have been fishing here since two. Neither of us has had a touch.

I am casting from the other side of pool. Like Howard, I am fishing from a flat ledge at the rim of the pool's downstream arc; like his, my waders are also bone dry. If I want, I can drop my Rusty Rat at Howard's feet; the pool is only fifty feet across. There is not room, really, for two of us to be working over such a small patch of water, but these are parlous times on the Leirasveit and serious adjustments must be made.

There may be a thousand Atlantic salmon in the pool at my feet. I have no way of counting; often I think there may well be more than a thousand. They are trapped here by Iceland's worst drought in almost fifty years. Since July, when most of these fish swam in from the sea two miles downriver, they have been held captive here by the falls. The volume of river water that drops some thirty feet in an almost vertical tumble is not enough to allow even the strongest fish its ascent. There is not enough substance for broad tails to push against. And the small depressions in the river-worn boulders that normally hold just enough water to give a salmon a perilous resting place halfway up the falls are barren saucers scummed with a dusty fretwork of sun-dried algae.

Denied their mortal and relentless compulsion to complete their life cycle, cut off from the fulfillment of their raging sexual imperatives and crazed by their crowding, one against the other in this pool that has shrunk from a hundred feet to fifty across and ebbed from its thirty-five-foot depth to less than twenty, the salmon have gone mad.

Milling incessantly at the foot of the falls, they thrash until one leaps silver in the sun, its tail whipping at air and froth, struggling for the propulsion that can move it against the tumbling water. Now and then, a fish contorted by panic will struggle halfway. Exhausted, it flops on bare rock. If I wanted, I could wait there and take my Icelandic salmon with two bare hands.

Incredibly durable, even out of its element, the salmon fibrillates and quivers in the open air, then slams its tail on the scummed, bare boulder and flips back into the falls, sliding on the edge of death back to the Home Pool's manic habitat.

I can see fish everywhere in the lower pool's cold, clear water. Much of the time, they are relatively calm, their gills opening and closing, their fins fanning as each holds its own slim cubic chamber, a self-imposed spacing that parks fish next to fish with just enough of the river between each to avoid actual contact. But whenever there is a hint of random disorder, when one salmon muscles another, or a single claustrophobic fish feels it can no longer hold motionless, a salmon will rocket across the pool until it reaches a barrier shore, then jump and hurtle on its demented surge. The palpable frustration of these explosions is contagious. Other fish in the pool cut loose, take off, and in moments the surface churns with the tormented spasms of creatures denied their implacable destiny.

It is both an awesome and tragic drama. On the one hand, I know I shall never see such numbers of these superlative fish so close at hand. On the other, I am shamed to be a voyeur of such desperation.

This is not what I thought we would witness when we traveled a thousand midsummer miles to this odd and exotic country. Yet perhaps I should have been ready for every exaggeration; this entire saga has been surreal from the start.

After our morning on the Kennebec, I did call Bob Manning and he put me in touch with Elisha Lee, a proper, old-money Bostonian who manages an enterprise called the Lee Family Office. It is Elisha who is the controling executive of the group that has arranged annual leases on the Leirasveit with the Icelandic sheep farmers who own the fishing rights. After dozens of phone calls as the broker between Elisha, Pritam, and a travel agent, the trip was, at last, arranged.

Jean and I, Brad, Howard Clifford and his wife Margaret, flew from Portland to Kennedy International Airport on Long Island where we met Pritam, his close friend Anne Johnston and her brother Alan. Pritam arrived just minutes before Icelandic Airways Flight 2202 was scheduled to take off on its overnight journey to the airport at Keflavik. We were relieved to see him; he had all our tickets and was the only one who knew precisely how we were going to get to the lodge on the river. He was very definitely our host; he had paid for each of our round-trip tickets and for our seven days of salmon fishing—the grand total comes to as much as the average Maine wage-earner makes in a year.

As the plane gained altitude over eastern Long Island, I could look down and see Georgica Pond, Three-Mile Harbor, Gardiner's Bay and Gardiner's Island, Cartwright Shoals, Montauk Point, and each of the other landmarks of my boyhood and early manhood, my first fishing years, my sinker-bouncing with Wyman, my snapper fishing with our first-born son, my embrace of my first striped bass . . . the setting sun etched each waterway of my past in golden bas-relief and I wondered as the plane droned into the long summer twilight at life's superb surprises. Each moment flows into every other and makes magic. As much as some of us might want to believe in constancy, there is none.

Look down at the vast emerald and pearl ice floes of Greenland there in the arctic dawn and tell me how I got here. I could say fish have cast my fate since I was born, but who would believe me?

A northern summer sun was already high in a morning sky when we landed at Keflavik just after six and it was afternoon when we reached the lodge on the meadow west of Borganes. A long, low, wood-frame building on a hillside that sloped toward the river, our fishing headquarters could have been one of the several, tidy white farmhouses in the Leirasveit valley.

Even though I hadn't slept in more than twenty-four hours, I walked along the scruffy dirt path that led from the lodge to the edge of the cliffs that overlooked Home Pool, even before Jean and I unpacked and made our nest in our small room with its two wooden bunks. The sixty-foot drop along the cliff's gravel face was high enough to give me a full view of the entire pool, the waterfall, and the stony spread of the low river as it trickled from the pool's deeper water across gravel bars so exposed I was certain no salmon could negotiate a passage.

When I first looked down I did not comprehend what I saw. No one had prepared me. The gently shifting dark shapes, so my standard references told me, were part of the river bottom, peculiar rock forms indigenous to this exotic land. But as I looked longer, I realized these were not inanimate shapes given movement by flowing water, but animate creatures. Fish! Salmon!

They had to be. But I had never seen salmon in such numbers. Never imagined such a gathering. Yet, from my promontory, with the sun above me opening the clear depths of the mountain river, I could not be mistaken.

Once my comprehension was certified, once I could lock to a new reference, I began to tabulate sizes. I could, I told myself, identify the grilse. They were the next-to-the-smallest shapes; those, I learned later, were sea trout. And I could mark several salmon that weighed at least thirty-five pounds or more, I was certain. Or they were sunken logs wedged in the rocks.

All doubt vanished in the silver rose that blossomed when a salmon leapt, hung suspended, and splashed in the pool's center. As it did, it upset the equilibrium of others finning in place. Startled, they surged toward safer space and as they moved their gleaming sides flashed luminous signals of such bright vitality the entire pool shivered with their force. For twenty minutes I bathed in the pool from sixty feet above, and those silent, silver crescendos seemed to ripple endlessly. I was too awed by the pageant, and too ignorant, to sense the panic I soon learned was there.

There are, according to the hand-drawn map of the eight miles of Leirasveit water that Elisha Lee leases, some thirty-five salmon pools that hold fish dependably enough to be cast over each day. With the river at its normal height, this gives anglers seven beats of some five pools each. With just six committed fisherpeople in our party, a healthy Leirasveit would have offered up more pools than we could handle.

As it was, of the thirty-five that might have been, we could fish only six, and these pools had become prisons.

For reasons that still elude me, I was not vexed or disappointed. Being in Iceland, and spending much of each day alone with Jean in the splendid and disarming solitude of that windswept space created an aura of romance and risk that moved us closer and closer until, alone on some vast sweep of barren volcanic rock our spirits embraced even though Jean sat placidly on the river bank studying a fragile blossom clinging to a boulder as I cast, thigh deep in the river.

That river was our guide, the road we traveled. Perhaps, if our pool was one of those a mile or more upstream, we would be driven there by Yap, the head guide and camp factotum. But unlike the guides at the Upsalquitch, who were each at the side of their angler throughout the long day, Yap would drop us at the nearest path to the river, give us a quick rundown on how we might best fish the pool, then wave goodbye, drive off in his van and leave us quite alone in some of the most dramatic and lonely landscapes I have ever walked.

Icelandic vistas are unique to the planet. The combined stress of active volcanos, vast reaches of cooled and sterile lava, underground thermal springs that are the national heat source, glaciers and their icy rivers, hills and mountains rising from the few green valleys those rivers generate, each of these combines with warm winds gentled by the Gulf Stream's meterological miracle and the twenty-two hours of daylight that floods a brief arctic summer to create an aura of mysticism and myth that casts a euphoric spell.

The entire island opens its treeless and rolling tundra to winds that circle each day like hawks, hunting along every valley, hurtling down every slope of every black and formidable hill, dashing across every meadow until they discover a Maine man trying to cast a fly into the wings of a gale. Those winds snatched curses from my mouth as easily as an osprey plucks a numbed herring from an icy spring freshet. Leaders tossed like chaff on the untrammeled gusts; much of my fishing time was spent crouched in the lee of some grotesque volcanic boulder pocked with porous gouges and twisted juts. There I sought shelter to replace a wind-knotted leader or tie on a new and different fly. As my eyes watered and the knots slipped impotently from my clumsy, numbed fingers, I would look across the stunning sweep of the treeless, rolling, Nordic hills, find Jean lying in a lee, her trim limbs flowing as easily as volcanic curves, and I would laugh at the surreal circumstance that brought us so wondrously together in this remote and startling land.

Stared at stupidly by the rumple-fleeced sheep that roam freely along every Iceland valley, and with a helpful demonstration by Yap, I developed what I call my Icelandic cast. No pretty, by-the-book, rod-high-and-loading strategy made sense on that turbulent moonscape. What you do, I told myself, is hold the rod at your hip, jerk it quickly back and forth, and then give it a sidearm thrust that zips the fly just above the bowed tops of the spindly grass and drops it in the center of the stream before the wind knows it's there. Lee Wulff would have a stroke if he were witness to the aberration, but even grace and good form are swept away by fifty-mile-an-hour gusts, especially if no one is watching.

Here at Home Pool the sidearm special can be kept under wraps. The cliffs that rise from both sides of this first major Leirasveit falls keep the winds at bay. With the afternoon sun spilling upstream, this small chasm is a warm, bright sanctuary. My Gore-Tex parka is folded on a boulder along with my heavy knit sweater of raw sheep's wool; both are standard equipment for most other pools on this and other Iceland rivers. It is the agreeable conditions that keep me at my casting more than any realistic hope. The notion that any of these tormented fish might show the slightest interest in a fly they have seen a hundred times is a thought difficult to sustain.

Howard, I observe, appears to be trying to snag his salmon. A slim, bearded, and rather grungy man in his late thirties, he reminds me a bit of Gabby Hayes as a young cowhand. It is, I think, the way Howard hops around the boulders, birdlike, peering into the white water, as if he can see the salmon he will hook. He has a bird's intensity, which is understandable, given the reputation he protects.

On a wall at L. L. Bean's twenty-four-hour sporting goods shopping extravaganza in Freeport, Maine, a large Atlantic salmon arches in the perpetual stress of a taxidermed leap. The thick, big-bellied fish, according to the legend etched on a brass plate bolted to the plaque, weighs something like thirty-seven-plus pounds and is the largest ever taken on a fly rod in a Maine river, or so the legend reads. It was caught by Howard Clifford of Portland, but the name of the river or stream where the battle took place does not appear.

This has been a source of some stress in Howard's life over the decade since his lucky day. A rather successful artist (he paints large, somewhat abstract landscapes that have a certain serene appeal) he is as well known, if not best known, as one of Maine's most controversial fishermen. Because he will not reveal the battle site, although he does say the fight lasted more than three hours, he and his salmon have been the topic of some serious cynicism.

One sports columnist has said several times he is convinced Howard caught his fish in New Brunswick or Quebec and then spirited it quickly across the border. Other rumblings sustain the notion that Howard plucked the trophy from the bootlegged catch of some illegal Kennebec gill netter. I have seen gill nets at the mouth of the river in June, and remember one that had at least three large salmon dead in its synthetic meshes.

My friend Herb Hartman, one of the few poets who ever served Maine as Parks Director, is a passionate but shy and quiet fly fisherman who has worked well and discreetly over the years to help strengthen the Atlantic salmon's tenuous hold on survival in Maine rivers. Herb, Lucy, and their sons live on the banks of the Sheepscot in an old Maine cape close to the Alna-Whitefield line. Their back yard slopes down a grassy hill to a fine Sheepscot pool, and Herb has told me several times of windless June nights when he can hear salmon tails slapping.

Like every serious salmon lover in the state, Herb has heard various versions of the Howard Clifford trophy story and he believes the artist made his catch in the Sheepscot, probably near Head Tide where a dam and falls slow migration and tend to concentrate the few fish that still navigate the river. I asked Howard about the Sheepscot site and he looked back at me blankly, although a half-smile slipped past his beard.

"Why don't you say where you got the fish?" I pressed. "Put an end to all this talk."

"I didn't tell when I first got the salmon because I didn't want everyone and his brother up there stomping around. And that's the same reason I have for not telling now." Howard's defense makes sense, but given the great

111

good fortune, dedication, and skill that it takes to catch a salmon anywhere in the Sheepscot, I doubt there will ever be any rush to its banks, trophy or no.

Howard, I think, is nourished by the controversy. His ego waxes each time the story is retold, each time one of the new curious makes his or her way to Bean's and asks how to find the wall where the great fish swims above the shoppers. It's something, to have your name next to a superfish. There's a massive blue marlin about twelve feet long that fills the back wall of the Full Moon Saloon in Key West. The 569-pound fish was taken, so the brass plate tells us, by Phil Caputo, a writer of deserved note, but surely known to hard drinkers in the Keys as the guy who caught that humungous fish.

So it is with Howard Clifford, and he has his status to keep at its current elevation, even here in Iceland, more than a thousand miles from the Sheepscot. He eyeballs me every now and then, making sure I'm not doing any better than he is and hoping, I surmise, that I'll give up and quit my casting so he can have Home Pool to himself.

I've changed flies several times, not because I know if one pattern will appeal but because I like the chance the ritual gives me to rest on a sun-warmed boulder and soak in some of the kindest and balmiest air Iceland has given us during this windy week. For once, on my first try I tie a decent knot to an Orange Blossom I bought from Jim Moores on the Upsalquitch.

I cast, just as I have cast for three hours now, across the pool. The fly sinks and moves downstream with the current until I begin to retrieve it, stripping in line slowly with my left hand, letting the loops drop to the flat ledge at my feet.

Pow! With a sudden, percussive splash, I am hooked to a salmon. At the very microsecond the fish discovers its error, chaos cascades through Home Pool.

My fish is across the pool before I can begin to cope with the slack in my line. Then, as I scramble, it takes off downstream, running off the flyline and taking a few yards of backing. But the dry streambed cannot be breached, even though the fish breaks my heart and certainly strains its as it thrashes vainly in less than an inch of water on a passage that once might have taken it to freedom.

Helped by the bend in my rod that pulls it toward the pool, the fish turns upstream and thrashes back to the deep water. This time, it heads straight for my feet and the ledge I stand on. For a moment, I'm convinced it will beach itself where I wait. Instead, it sounds at the ledge and takes my line at an angle directly below me but even farther toward the shore.

My rock, I know now, is an outcrop, a jutting ledge that slants upward and outward from the river bottom. In the submerged cave the formation creates, the salmon finds shelter. I try to dislodge it, shaking my rod tip, banging the rod with my hand, and putting so much strain on the line I am certain the six-pound leader will snap. The fish appeared to be about a ten-pounder when I saw it in the thin water downstream.

Howard has scrambled around and is at my side, chirping encouragement and trying so hard to be a good sport about my hook-up (as opposed to his) that he convinces me. I am, I have learned, always ready to be convinced whenever any human being displays a semblance of manners. I long so for what is good in each of us.

Howard got here quickly, I tell myself. Perhaps I can get to the opposite side just as fast. From that angle I should be able to tug the stubborn fish from its holding cave. Stepping carefully across water-worn rocks with my rod held high above my head, I let line slip off the reel on a light drag. Once across, I tighten the drag and bend back until

113

the rod trembles. At the moment I am certain the line will snap, the salmon relents and cuts upstream again and heads directly for the white water at the base of the falls. As the fish moves, I can feel the thumps of others against the taut line.

Except for my consciousness of this salmon, my intellect is as empty, as clear as a crystal ball. This totality of focus takes over whenever a fish and I make contact, whoever the fish, wherever we meet. My world is cemented by the connection the line makes between me and the wild creature. My planet is as large as the stretch of water that separates us, one from the other. I have never thought of these meetings as battles; I do not see myself as "fighting" a fish. We compete, yes. But we do not fight; it is not possible, just as it is not possible for a man and woman who love each other. They may compete, but they do not fight.

I sometimes ask myself if it is rational to become so intimate and totally involved with a finned soul swimming, but I never pursue the answer. Why should I? The captivation is too total, the experience too absorbing.

If the fish does not escape, if it is not the first to break off our affair, then the world returns. If, as this salmon does, the fish begins to quit the struggle, I begin to regret any discomfort I have brought it. And when the fish slides into shallow water and is clearly exhausted, my impulse is to set it free.

But we have been told Icelandic regulations require us to keep every fish we land. The salmon will be sold, according to our guidebooks, and the proceeds shared with the farmer who owns the meadows along the Leirasveit's banks.

As I slide this salmon into the shallows I learn it has not been fairly hooked. Instead of in its jaw, my Orange Blossom is stuck in the ridge of gristle just in front of the

114

salmon's tail. I have read that these fish sometimes slap at a fly with their tails. They are irritated by the fly's presence, so they knock it away.

That's what has happened here. That, or I snagged the fish simply because there are so many jammed in this pool. Howard, who has, I know, been tempted to snag one, is quite pleased with my misfortune. I have, in his eyes, set a pattern which he can now follow with less chance of criticism.

In spite of how it was hooked, the fish is lovely: solid, well shaped, and silver—a salmon still fresh from the sea.

It is almost seven. The sun has begun to ride lower in the western sky, but there are still four hours until it sets. I walk up the gravel path toward the lodge where Jean waits for me at the fence. She sees the fish, runs to get her camera, and when I get to the gate she asks me to stop and pose, holding the salmon high and out, still in my waders, the rod angling against the sky from my hand. The sun is gold at my back. A wash of golden light spills over us and the hills around us, the hills that hold the Leirasveit and its salmon in the rolling curve of their windswept arms.

Sanibel, Florida

March 19, 1985

———

his Florida modification
of the traditional red-headed and white-bodied plug that has
been used for a century by fresh and salt-water fishermen
casts like a dream. It is making me look as good as Lefty
Kreh because its density and weight are right for the slim
spinning rig I'm using, and because here in this soft, windless air I can toss it more than a hundred feet with an easy
flick of my wrist.

But my form is not impressing the fish, if indeed there
are any here in this channel that flows between Sanibel Island and the Florida mainland less than a mile across the
water due east. Sanibel's landmark lighthouse, a graceful,
romantic relic of the age of navigation by compass, sextant
and timepiece (as opposed to high-tech electronics) is a few
hundred yards south from the slim strip of sand under my
bare feet.

We are, Jean and I, in a quasi-public park where we
have come each evening since we arrived on this west coast
island three days ago. There may be two acres here, surely
no more. It is one of those rare places left on either the

117

Atlantic or the Gulf coast of this beleagured state. Someone had the good sense to set this point aside, to save the lighthouse and the native trees, shrubs and plants that twine and rise so vigorously from water's edge to water's edge. This is how all of the island and much of Florida once was: a formidable natural presence, a mass of vegetation, green and reaching with the sinewed arms of its roots and its bristling limbs to force any invader to pay a heavy toll in the hard currency of sweat and exertion. That was before bulldozers, before clam-shell dredging buckets and front-end loaders, before developers discovered the true fragility of a landscape that had once appeared so formidable. One sweep of a 'dozer blade, one touch of a match to a brush pile, and in days the bare marl would be leveled and ready for beach-front condominiums rising like fast-growing corn in a fertile field.

We walked to this patch of what once was from a condominium down the road, a comfortable place on the Gulf beach that belongs to Allen and Gertrude McCue, good friends and fellow croquet enthusiasts from Maine. They need their Volvo driven north from here, and I quickly said of course we would do it when they offered their place to me and Jean for a week in return for the driving. There is no March fishing in Maine and, besides, Florida's soft air and its caressing waters are presences that have beckoned since I first discovered the state forty-five years ago, courtesy of the Army Air Corps.

The spinning rod that responds so well to my casting form is borrowed, yet another reason for the contentment of this place, this evening, this entire Sanibel experience.

The rod belongs to Erhard "Matty" Matthiessen, a true and gentle gentleman who now spends much of his time at his home on Captiva, the smaller island to the north linked to Sanibel by causeway. He was properly surprised when I phoned him. We had not seen each other since the fall of 1948, the year that Matty changed my life. And, I'm quite certain, the year I also changed his—mine for the better, his for the not-quite-so-good.

After my discharge from the Air Corps in the fall of 1945, after I spurned their gilded lies about what a fine career awaited if I continued to fly aboard heavy bombers, I returned to Yale, the college I had entered as a freshman just out of prep school five years earlier. I joined the Air Corps just before Yale kicked me out. I had not been as lucky at prep school.

Boys-only boarding schools may be right for some adolescents, but I found five years of lonely discipline at Woodberry Forest a crushing repression. Without the newly discovered joys of masturbation and an endless capacity for vivid sexual fantasy, I might never have stayed. As it was, I got caught climbing the back stairs on the dawn before my graduation with a bottle of champagne in my hand. I was returning from a Richmond country club dance for the girls of St. Catherine, lured there by a southern teaser who had given me nothing more than a stony erection and a kiss on the cheek.

Mr. Lord (Creeping Jesus to us boys) was coming down those stairs as I was going up. I have never learned what suspect errand brought him my way at five A.M., but my parents, who had traveled by rail from Manhattan to watch me get my diploma, were properly disgruntled when I told them I had been expelled earlier in the day at a curt ceremony in the headmaster's office.

Today, with my secondary-school record (between us, my brother Chick and I served more time for more demerits than any of the school's 220 students) I would be lucky to find a spot at a second-rate vocational school. But 1940 is far back in the rapidly evolving world of higher edu-

119

cation. Allowed to take my College Board exams at Woodberry, I did well enough to be granted conditional
admission to Yale's Class of '45.

After one day in Wright Hall on the Old Campus I had
the place cased. No one was watching! I could come and go
as I pleased, and I did. Like a star shell fired from a gun that
had been loaded for five years, I exploded high over the
campus.

I had run the mile for Woodberry's track team, an
effort that meant I could not drink or smoke and had to
spend much of my time training. At Yale, athletics were not
compulsory. Drinking and smoking were allowed, and
fashionable. I tried, between September 22 when I moved in
to Wright Hall, and December 7 when Pearl Harbor offered
me a gentleman's exit from under a cloud, to loosen each of
the cramps those five years at boarding school had knit in
my libido.

Puking kept me in shape. The dynamic tensions my
system endured as I bent taut over toilets tossing back the
excess of the previous night's drinking maintained my mus-
cle tone. But the sessions seldom prepared me for class. By
the time the first grading period became inevitable, I had
two Fs and an X—a rare ranking at Yale—and a letter from
the Dean of Students that all but detailed my bleak future as
a former Yale man.

Which led me to the Army Air Corps mobile recruiting
station conveniently parked on College Street just a step
from the Old Campus.

It was the sentimental rush of good feeling that the ci-
vilian population accorded its returning combat veterans
that swayed the Dean's otherwise good judgment and let
me re-enter Yale four years and thirty-five missions later.
And perhaps it was the forced maturity those missions im-

posed that kept me reasonably alert and able to graduate in June 1948—the year Matty Matthiessen changed my life.

I did not attend that Yale graduation. I had my diploma mailed because the job Matty offered me at Fisher's Island was set to begin as soon as I could possibly get there. That was after my last exam at Yale, not after the commencement rituals which were scheduled ten days later. So I missed my second, and last, graduation.

The opportunity was worth it. As a well-rooted resident of Fisher's Island and a practicing architect, Matty had been asked to restore the island's vast masonry and turreted country club to its pre-war grandeur and social excitement. Not only was he the structural repairman, but he was the man charged with organizing a lifestyle that would allow the island's well-heeled summer residents and Fisher's Island Country Club members to make believe that neither the war nor the New Deal had ever happened.

My job, which five years at Woodberry and almost four at Yale had definitely not prepared me for, was running the brand-new country-club launch: a twenty-one-foot, trunk-cabin, sparkling white Chris-Craft twin-screw speedster powered by two 90-horsepower inboard engines. She was a holdover from prohibition days, a small boat beautifully built for speed, trimmed in graceful mahogany brightwork, outfitted with a proper ship's steering wheel and the immediate responses of a thoroughbred. For my kind of fellow in those days, she was quite certainly my kind of boat.

Why, of all the young men, almost any of them more stable and less reckless than I, did Matty choose me to skipper the club's newest and most expensive amenity?

I have never been sure of the answer, and I have never asked him.

His son, Peter, a classmate of mine at Yale, had some influence, I'm certain. Partly because I was enamored of a young lady in New Canaan and partly because I felt so comfortable with the warmth and good spirits of the Matthiessen's handsome home in the Stamford countryside, I often spent weekends there, leaving New Haven's football games and drinking bouts for a peaceful Saturday and Sunday sixty miles south on the Merritt Parkway. Peter and I were both fishermen, bird hunters, and curious amateur naturalists who enjoyed almost any activity that took us outdoors. During the summers, Peter was a frequent visitor to East Hampton where we shared several excursions on Gardiner's Bay and some macabre duck shooting on illegal evenings.

Because Peter and I so often shared small boats on these coastal episodes, he assumed I knew my way around the water. At least I have always thought that's what he told his father. Matty, a tall, blue-eyed man with a wide and frequent smile, harbored a quiet amusement, a fine and great good humor about life—an adventure, in his view, to be enjoyed. And he found much amusement in the thought that I could be skipper of a boat ferrying some of America's most wealthy and powerful folks. He knew he was taking a gamble on me, and that was the fun of it.

He came mortally close to losing all his chips. I could row a skiff, sail small sloops, and manage an outboard, but I'd never docked a powerboat or navigated after dark. But I was supremely discreet about these gaps in my mariner's experience. Instead, I initiated a self-education process that would, I hoped, bring me up to snuff before my shortcomings were realized. Using the cramming systems I'd learned so well at Yale, I studied hard for the U.S. Coast Guard examination that would, if I passed, earn me the papers that certified me a skipper qualified to carry passengers for hire aboard motor vessels less than sixty-five feet long in coastal waters. Preparing for that exam took many more hours than the total I needed to get decent grades on my Yale finals.

I passed. There I was, full of juice, Humphrey Bogart in *To Have and Have Not* at the wheel of an overpowered launch that could hit thirty knots without breathing hard. There I was, young, single, horny, thirsty, and living free in a house by the sea on an island twenty miles north of Montauk Point and three miles southeast of New London, an island summer-peopled with lithe ladies whose husbands toiled in Cleveland and Manhattan, tan, long-limbed college girls who knew the rules of summer romance, carte blanche at the club bar and restaurant, my grandfather's 1938 Packard, bluefish off Race Rock and striped bass in every curling cove along that magic island's rocky shore. If pleasure were wine, I would have passed out the first week.

As it was, I came close to losing my commission. Towing a Rockefeller brother on water skis, I whipped through Watch Hill Harbor one placid Sunday afternoon, demonstrating to my distinguished client that I knew as well as anyone how to show a water skier a good time. In and out of the moored yachts and yawls we went, careening, twisting, roaring up a storm. Gold bracelets laughed on bronze arms waved by sleek nymphs cheering from my decks as I powered the launch a few reckless feet from the stern of a ninety-foot yacht where ladies in wide hats were gathered on the fantail for tea.

A few days later, the club's lawyer asked me to stop by his office. Like so many of the Fisher's Island folk, he headed one of Wall Street's most impressive firms when he wasn't summering on the Sound. White-haired, judicial, and grim he told me the club was being sued by the owner of a yacht that had been moored in Watch Hill Harbor the weekend just past.

"Were you towing a water skier inside the harbor?" he asked, his elderly blue eyes large with alarm at what he hoped would not be the answer.

"Yes sir." I had no notion of what was coming.

"Well," he paused, gathering strength for the grim business, "we have a problem. Your wake rolled enough Dresden china off that yacht's tea table to add up to about $1,200. Our insurance doesn't cover that sort of negligence.

"John," he said, his eyes firing, "what do you expect us to do?"

I was, I suppose, expected to suggest they find someone more disciplined to skipper their launch. But the thought never even took shape. I was on another tack entirely.

"Where's the bill for the tea set?" I asked. "I'll pay it." That's the sort of summer it was. I was making so much money on the profit-sharing formula Matty had designed that I could come up with $1,200 in cash, no problem.

Because the lawyer, and Matty, for all I know, had made a prior decision to fire me, the response to my offer was a long pause. "I'll see if that's agreeable with the various interested parties," were the words the attorney came up with. In the euphoria of that incredible summer, I never even guessed how close I had come to the edge of the precipice.

Adventure followed adventure as I rocketed on. I ferried Admiral Bull Halsey's daughter and granddaughter from the island across to Watch Hill one night in a wooly fog that had me bent over my compass praying that I could follow the instructions the Admiral gave me as I pulled away from the club dock. "You get them there in good shape, captain," the hero of the Pacific Navy told me and I knew the entire Seventh Fleet would be on my ass if I didn't.

I negotiated the twisting Watch Hill channel and eased into the yacht club dock as if I'd done it a thousand times. It was, I thought, too foggy to return so I walked up the street to the Harkness mansion and announced myself as John Cole's son. Graciously, my father's friend Bill Harkness took me in and joined me in a scotch and soda served in a crystal glass so thin I could have crushed it with a single squeeze.

It was that sort of summer. I cruised to Manhasset with Jock Whitney aboard his breathtaking *Aphrodite,* a speed yacht still revered by international boat lovers. I had dinner with Hugh Chisolm in the oak-paneled dining salon of his *Aras,* a yacht built with the proceeds of the Chisolm paper mills in Maine. And I took Joe Pulitzer bluefishing off Race Rock. We had a fine day and at its close he asked me what I would do when the summer ended.

"I want to be a reporter," said I.

And he, bubbling with the electric effervescence of a light-aired late-August afternoon and three nine-pound bluefish in the ice chest said, "Come to Saint Louis and try the *Post-Dispatch.*"

Which I did much later in the year.

It was that kind of summer. And through its sapphire weeks and luminous night, Matty Matthiessen was there, his eyes glowing with amusement as brightly as dewdrops in the rising sun. He forgave my transgressions and tolerated my excesses. We shook hands when I left, each of us knowing success had outweighed failure, the good had overcome the bad, and the fates of both of us had been kind to the point of indulgence. He never once welcomed me with anything but his warm and blinding smile, never once allowed reality to smother mischief's delights.

125

And now, thirty-seven years later, I hold Matty's fishing rod in my hands. I have a piece of him still with me. And when I went with Jean to his home in Captiva to pick up the rod and he opened the door, his smiling eyes and his big smile were there waiting, carried across the years by the man's exuberant love for life.

That summer . . . the embrace of this soft evening . . . Matty . . . Sanibel . . . what gifts the fish have given.

Aboard MV *Delaware*

November 22, 1963

A hand shakes my shoulder. The cabin is dark, I cannot see who is doing the shaking. Some light squeezes past the half-open cabin door from the narrow corridor, but not enough.

My responses are slow, confused. My sleep has been deep, the cabin quite dark in the dusk of this November evening. I have no notion of how long I've slept. Perhaps I am being shaken awake to get to the ship's mess in time for supper.

In the ten days I have been aboard the *Delaware* I have learned many lessons, one especially well: do not raise your head from your pillow when you awaken.

My upper bunk in this cramped four-bunk stateroom is no more than eight inches under the steel-plate of the vessel's deck that's just above me. The steel, bulging with rivets, is consistently unforgiving. Even though it creaks and screams in the stress of the North Atlantic's angry combers, it does not yield one millimeter when my head cracks against it. For forty years I have awakened unrestrained, able to sit up, raise my arms, or, if the day is golden before me, leap from my bed to greet it.

The *Delaware* has taught me otherwise. I have the lesions of my lessons. I do not rise up on one elbow and turn toward my guest, whoever he may be and whatever his mission. Instead, as my consciousness makes its way through the miasma of my first truly sound sleep in ten days. I turn my head carefully toward the bunk's outer edge, blink my eyes as I work to get them to focus on the head silhouetted against the light beyond the cabin door. My visitor's voice is a presence, but not yet decipherable. I hear sounds but cannot yet convert them to words with any meaning.

I can, however, sense some alarm, some urgency in the tone. That gets my adrenalin piping a bit and I can feel my reflexes begin to accelerate. Aboard the *Delaware,* the sensation is a familiar one. I have been dangling above the chasm of helpless anxiety ever since I came aboard on Armistice Day.

November 11: Veteran's Day now, but Armistice Day when Chick and I were first sent to boarding school at Friends Academy in Locust Valley, Long Island. I was ten and Chick nine; we were two of the school's fourteen boarders and we roomed together and fought together, wrestling with the desperation of our needs, finding a bitter reassurance in the distress we caused each other with our full nelsons, scissor grips across the belly, hammer locks, and every other painful embrace that eased the distress of our aloneness.

In the general silence of the several daily assemblies in the Quaker school, where silence was a blessed form of worship, the silence at eleven o'clock on the morning of November eleventh was particularly memorable. Students, faculty, adminstrative staff, the entire Friends Academy

128

complement would be gathered in the cavernous (to a ten-year-old) study hall and asked by Principal Blackburn to observe a minute of silence in memory of those who had fallen during the Great War.

Most often, I thought of our Uncle John, a Navy pilot during the Great War. He had not fallen. He visited his sister, our mother, often, and showed up almost every Sunday for the family dinners at the big table set with silver and fine china. When Uncle John arrived, we would study each of his moves and gestures, trying to learn if he had already had "a bit too much to drink," as our mother put it.

Those Sunday vignettes popped up for still another showing thirty years later when Jean and I drove from Brunswick to Gloucester on Veterans Day, 1963, and I spent considerable time explaining to her why I still called it Armistice Day.

Our situation called for light conversation of no consequence. I was so desperately in love. And Jean, a widow with four children, tried to cope with the persistence of my presence. Together in every sense of the word, but not yet sanctified in convention's lexicon, we were on the brink of our first separation since our liaison had begun. In keeping with the lifelong imbalance of my exaggerated emotionalism, I was treating the prospect of a two-week cruise aboard the *Delaware* as if I had been ordered to join the garrison at Khyber Pass. In the terrible intensity of those first months of our relationship, every separation defined the possibility of permanent loss, and the prospect of two weeks in the North Atlantic in late November aboard a beam trawler with fifty-eight years of wear on her rusty plates held enough genuine reasons for concern to give a rational man pause. At the time, I was not a rational man.

So why had I gone to considerable efforts to arrange the voyage? Fish. What else?

Built at the Bath Iron Works (how circumstance tumbles) in the years just after that Great War, when more warships were decidely not on the Navy's agenda, the *Delaware* was the first move in the Iron Works' peacetime strategy. Larger beam trawlers capable of the longer trips needed to make a profit in the overfished waters of the North Atlantic were much in demand as peace was declared and offshore commercial fishing resumed.

Because high hopes went down the ways with her, and because the Iron Works does indeed build worthy ships, the *Delaware* aged well. During World War II, she was acquired by the Navy for patrols and mine-sweeping, and when peace was once again declared, she transferred to the Bureau of Marine Fisheries. By the time she and I had our meeting, the *Delaware* served in the Bureau's Exploratory Gear and Research branch with Gloucester as her home port and the North Atlantic as her primary testing ground for new developments in fish-catching equipment.

Long-lining—the business of setting hundreds of baited hooks hung from a single line often more than a mile long—was being blamed for depleting several major sports-fishing stocks, especially billfish like marlin and swordfish. In my view, I could combine yet another fishing adventure with a chance to learn more about long-lining and its effect on the resource. And, as a lifelong opponent of any and all bureaucracies, I also wanted a first-hand look at how the U.S. Bureau of Marine Fisheries did its work in my neck of the ocean.

The tedious arrangements with the federal government were made months before my romance with Jean began boiling over. Nevertheless, in my view, there was nothing for it but to honor my commitment and make the trip. Fish were victorious once again.

The price I paid, however, was pegged at the outer limits of emotional stability.

Armistice Day was clear, blue, and wrenching. In the azure clarity of a New England autumn, Jean waved from the dock at Gloucester until the *Delaware* turned the corner at the port's long breakwater and set her course for an invisible merging of oceanic currents some four hundred miles north-northeast of Cape Cod. I stood at the rail waving back until we reached cruising speed in the open sea and the Atlantic's heavy autumnal swells began the rhythmic heaving that would be a constant presence in our short days and long, long nights.

Most of the crew, including the skipper, were Italian Americans and Portuguese, the primary population of Gloucester and the third and fourth generation of its fishermen. Discouraged by the increased costs of running their own draggers and the radically reduced stocks of food fish on what was once the world's most productive fishing grounds, the men had sold out and gotten jobs doing the same work, but this time for government paychecks, pensions, and health insurance.

They had to give up being their own men and the general tenor aboard the *Delaware* was a kind of bored resignation. If the researchers did stumble across a new, rich fishery, this crew would not share the benefits as they would aboard their own boat. They missed the excitement of anticipation, that incredibly persistent vision of plenty that every fisherman must have; without it, he would be a bricklayer or shopkeeper. And because they could not anticipate, they looked for other diversions.

One was newcomers aboard. And I was the only one. Thus each day I was told in lurid detail of the vessel's inherent capacity for disaster.

"She come close to breaking right in two last time we was out, didn't she, Joe?" The engineer fed lines to the first mate who sat in the wheelhouse high chair, the one just behind the electronic and manual controls that governed the *Delaware*'s speed and course. A talkative and rather light-hearted Italian, the first mate alternated watches on the bridge with the captain, a remote and silent man who seldom shared even the most perfunctory greetings with me. As I began to get in tune with the four-hours-on and four-off rhythms of the ship's watches, I made my visits to the bridge when I knew Joe would be at the wheel.

But even his natural warmth could not keep him from joining the engineer's fright games. "We get a good nor'wester in this cold water," Joe said remorselessly, "and she hits one of them seas just right, there's going to be rivets rattling on that deck like bolts in a tin bucket. Why this tub should have been retired years ago. We ain't going to have a chance when she does come apart.

"Bang! She's going to go all of a sudden. Ain't nobody going to have time to get to those two rust buckets they call lifeboats there on the stern. We'll all go down together, won't we old girl?"

In the long, dark silence of the eight-to-midnight watch, I waited for the engineer's voice to float from the far corner of the wheelhouse where he sat on a stool, his back wedged against the corner's right angle. But no words of reassurance took flight to rout the terrors already scaling the walls of my common sense. Instead, I stood beside Joe, looking for some response from him, there in the luminous green shadows of the binnacle light. As I leaned into the wheelhouse bulkhead, bracing against the ship's pitching and pounding, I could see the luminous tops of combers roaring in silence beyond the bow. Overhead, stars sparked hard in the cold, moonless sky, making a mockery of the serenity they would have signified had I been ashore. Here they were a brutal irony, removed in space, unwilling and unable to exert any control over a sea that did precisely as it pleased, slamming the *Delaware* with a slap amidships, cuffing her about the bow, and dumping green ice water on her 'midships work deck so when I looked down from the bridge at night I could imagine the ship had already surrendered her precarious buoyancy.

"I'm going below," the engineer said at last. "Those engines don't sound too good. Could blow any minute."

He went straight to the galley for coffee, but I spent the next half-hour listening to the vibrations of the ship's huge diesels, taut with my aural search for any anomaly in their endless hum.

On the third night, the attacks on my psyche were called off. Joe, the engineer, and the others in the crew who had assembled their armies of prevarication and exaggeration decided I was not going to buckle and therefore was no longer a worthy target. I was left alone on the bridge with Joe, and our routine scripts took quite a different turn.

"Christ, coffee makes me horny, don't it you?"

That was Joe's opening salutation each evening as I clambered to the bridge, and our conversation seldom got more profound. "Fried eggs, now there's nothing makes a man hornier than fried eggs. Did you know that?" That was how Joe would close our dialogues when his watch ended and we sat together in the midnight silence of the galley and he enjoyed his meal: fried eggs and black coffee. How he held himself in check after such excess I never inquired.

I would leave him, head aft toward my bunk, and try to sleep. Perhaps it was all the coffee I had downed, keeping Joe company. Or it was the thumping of the anxieties I still harbored, but had not allowed to surface. Whatever the causes, and they also included the steel deck inches above

133

my nose, I seldom slept. Instead, I lay rigid on my back, while my waking dreams roared past like express trains on their way to nowhere and I waited for the *Delaware* to implode on that merciless and gigantic wave I knew was out there one thin, rusty, steel plate away from where I lay prone, trapped, and helpless.

I would be up before dawn, waiting for the day's work to begin.

As it does in most government enterprise, routine played the leading role in the *Delaware*'s research efforts. First the captain, in concert with the presiding marine biologist from the Woods Hole Oceanographic Institute, would agree on where we were. Given our solitude in the northern reaches of the planet's most restless winter ocean, the matter of pinpointing our position required considerable effort and sophisticated technology. With the help of radioed navigational bearings, electronic marvels like Loran, and sensitive water temperature readings, the ship would be positioned over a mid-Atlantic thermocline: the invisible meeting place of a cold-water mass with a warmer one. It was here, according to theory, that fish gathered. In my imagination, they waited on the warm side finning gently in place, waiting for shrimp or some equally abundant food to come swimming through from the cold mass, stupid with numbness and ready to be eaten without the trouble of a chase.

Once the invisible thermocline was determined, the ship's few crew members would gather at one side of the stern, ready to set the several tubs of baited hooks. In contrast to the imagined perils of the *Delaware*'s instant disintegration, setting long-line gear from a vessel originally designed as beam trawler was definitely hazardous duty. A slip, a tangle, an unexpected pitch or roll, and one of the fist-sized stainless-steel hooks could bury itself in a forearm or thigh. To be removed at sea, it would have to be pushed and turned through the flesh until the barbed point emerged and could be snipped with wire cutters. No such accidents happened while I was aboard, but I was told of other hookings on other trips and I believed those reports. Anyone who watched the intricate process involving so many hundreds of hooks and what looked like insoluble tangles of stiff polypropylene line would have to know that sooner or later blood would flow.

When the miles of gear were set, the *Delaware* would steam to the spot on that gray and trackless sea where the first marker had been heaved overboard hours before. The small flag buoy of gleaming metal mesh reflected its own unique blip on the ship's radar screen, electronically leading us back to where we began.

After the marker was retrieved and the first hooks began coming over the gunwale and through the pulley wheel of the haulback system, I was the only man aboard without a job. As supercargo, staying out of the way was my first responsibility. I chose a fine location. A narrow catwalk framed the front and sides of the bridge. Protected by its chest-high steel rail, I could lean far over and watch every move made on the working deck ten feet below. As winches stressed the long line from its lair six, eight, ten, or even twenty fathoms down, I could tell by the tension and tugging whether there was a fish of any consequence hooked on the mute traps set a few hours before.

Sharks were able to endure the captivity in relative good health and were often a violent problem for the crew. Endowed with a superbly primitive design for survival, sharks would fight for their lives as they were hauled from the sea. Tails thrashing, jaws snapping, bulky torsos contorting and rolling, they tangled yards of line around their muscular bodies, forcing the *Delaware* and her haul-back

135

rhythm to a halt while the crew beat the shark about the head with shortened baseball bats and tried to free up the surprisingly tangled skeins the creature had woven. Often this meant cutting the line, yet another risky maneuver on the wet and pitching steel decks.

Freed, every shark was slid forward to the biologists for inspection and analysis. From my perch, I was most impressed with the younger of the two Woods Hole scientists: a tall, lanky, dark-haired and dark-eyed man named Martin Bartlett who seemed anxious to establish a kind of rapport with every fish, including the sharks, that came over the rail. Marty, I decided, after watching him work a day or so, was almost as unbalanced as I. He loved fish, all fish.

He had, I was certain, been measuring, weighing, and analyzing the stomach contents of fish hauled aboard the *Delaware* for several years, but he still greeted each new arrival with a wonderful and zany enthusiasm. He would yelp with joy when some exotic creature of the depths slid his way, its eyes popped out by the trauma of the violent pressure shift that also inverted its stomach and left it dangling from its mouth like some grotesque tongue. As precisely as a chief surgeon in his operating room, and stolidly unperturbed by the grotesqueries of rapid pressure change, Marty made his notes and measurements.

Every now and then the crew would toss back a tropical anomaly brought by the Gulf Stream's eddies to this North Atlantic thermocline: a crimson fish with chrome yellow fins, or a bit of sapphire exotica sporting pendulous dangles from its wide lower jaw. Because he knew of my addiction, Marty would look up from his work, hold the fish high so I could see it in the full colors of its emergence, colors that would fade as life left. Behind the arm that stretched with enthusiasm and the hand that held the tidbit I would see Marty's remarkable smile flashing like some solitary, joyous beacon there in that dun and rusty work space busied by men of grim visage concentrating on staying clear of random hooks, remorseless machinery, and a relentless sea always determined to verify its dominance.

Heightened by the contrast of his tanned and weather-beaten visage, Marty's fine white teeth reflected his bright spirit, a boy leapt from the man as charged with a zest for life as a child on Christmas morning. Whatever extremes the sea might impose, whatever discomforts the *Delaware* kept on demand, Marty was ready and willing to accept. In return, he could awaken each morning in his bunk certain of the immediacy of the sky, the sea, and the enchantments of each of its countless living organisms from protozoa to whales, from sharks to sunfish.

Neither the human nor electronic fish-finders aboard the *Delaware* had much success locating swordfish or other billfish, one of the priority goals of our exploratory cruise. But one gray forenoon as the Atlantic did its implacable best to keep the vessel's decks awash in white water, a rather small swordfish that I judged to be about a 150-pounder turned up on the line and Marty's grin was broader, more playful than ever. The fish, like most of its brethren, had been killed by its captivity. Struggling to escape the hook that restrained it, the swordfish had fought until it died. But sharks had not yet discovered the corpse and Marty had a fine specimen to examine. When he finished, he sawed off the long sword and brought it to me on the bridge. I'd told him I hoped I could have one as a memento of the voyage.

Together we talked about how to process the symmetrical bit of bone, how to preserve and enhance it and fashion and attach a proper handle. As we talked, Marty came to know of Jean, her children, and my emotional affliction. Neither glib nor overserious in response, he laughed with the joy of meeting another male given to ro-

137

mantic extremism. Nourished by the vicarious passion he sensed, he further encouraged it by explaining to me that I could, if I wanted, use the ship's radio-telephone to call Jean from the bridge.

That evening around nine he joined Joe at the helm and as I waited in the wavering dark, together they chattered with the ship-to-shore operator and within a half-hour handed me a receiver that somehow brought me Jean's gentle voice from her kitchen phone in Brunswick, Maine.

The *Delaware*'s radio-telephone was precisely that, and the radio half was dominant. Simultaneous two-way conversation was not possible; when I wanted to talk, I first had to push a button on my hand-held transmitter; when I wanted to listen, I released the button. Like some uncoordinated puppy so eager to get to his supper he spills the entire dish, I tried to talk too much. But, forgetting to press the button, I would be shouting into a mute mouthpiece while Jean would be calling my name, seeking some response. Meanwhile, atmospheric vagaries sometimes dissolved what communication we could establish. A subway kind of sound would fill my ears and Jean would vanish in the voids of space.

Unable to contain myself, I pressed the button in a vise grip and began shouting "I love you! I love you!" as loudly and strenuously as I could, as if my voice alone might span the five hundred miles of darkness. When I realized the excess of my compulsion and let go, I heard Jean's voice say, "I love you, too."

Then it was time to end it. I could take no more tightening of the emotional rack. As I handed the receiver to Marty, his vast grin illuminated the wheelhouse. He put his arm around Joe and two grins merged.

"That was real nice, wasn't it, Joe?" Marty said. "Romance at sea. How I miss it.

138

"John," he said, "someday I want to meet your lady. And now that you've had some practice, we'll try another call tomorrow. It helps the time go faster for me and Joe, don't you know."

"But I think I better tell the skipper and the crew what's we're doing," the first mate said. "The way you're yelling, the whole ship can hear. They might think you're talking to me."

Yesterday, the northwest wind came at us in gusts that topped thirty knots. From a clear sky, the gale chopped the sea in stubby sections of ice water topped with spindrift blown like salt snow across empty decks and lashed equipment. With no work possible, and with the *Delaware* idling into the seas, rising, falling, slamming, and yawing, and every so often shuddering in the creamy trough of a towering swell topped with waves of its own, the hours dragged at edge of panic and through the center of boredom. When I began to resent my bunk, the confines of the steel-walled cabin, and the bolts just above my nose, I went up on deck and let the gale slap at the hood of my slicker drawn tight around my cheeks.

Alone in the wind's booming careen, I clung to the rail and watched wide-eyed as seas that seemed about to sweep me from my feet slid instead under the *Delaware*'s plump stern, lifting the ship as easily as a giant hand might heft a well-rounded ass. This was a November gale sailing on the force of a vast high pressure system—wind without weather, seas without a storm.

And under the afternoon sun low in the late-autumn sky, the wind-tossed sea sparkled in countless refractions of the gale's violence. Quite suddenly, a pod of whales, humpbacks I thought, surfaced off the port quarter, less than two hundred feet from where I watched, amazed and alone.

At the center of that chill universe, they gamboled at some gargantuan game that at first I could not comprehend. But I knew theirs was not a random recess; there was a sense of purpose in their movements, a stubborn effort made to stay together in this one anonymous meeting place.

When one whale rolled almost on his back, exposing his underside, I thought I understood. The whale's great penis, a pale limb sprung from a huge, dark tree, swayed naked for a moment, then vanished as the creature swung upright, its black back awash. Turning as if tethered to a fixed point, the group stayed alongside the idling *Delaware* for almost an hour, and although I never glimpsed such documentary evidence again, it became clear that a female whale, or perhaps two, was at the center of the loose circle of behemoths, being courted by a half-dozen males whose final stages of leviathan lovemaking I did not witness. Or, if I did, the lovemaking was too covert for me to certify.

Nevertheless, the notion that even unrequited love could be made on the icy surface of such a wind-tossed sea somehow heartened me, eased my claustrophobia, moved me to a level of meditation and calm that allowed me to rejoice in the magnificence of the elements around, above, and below me rather than railing against them.

As if to reward me for my new awareness of her mystery, the sea gave me yet another gift before the day ended. An hour or so after the whales had vanished, lost to me forever in the sea's vast cave, I saw the largest school of dolphin I had ever seen. Again, at first sight I was unaware of the real nature of my vision. On the western horizon, against a sun now almost setting, it appeared as if the ocean had grown a fringe. Slim columns of spray bent like pale fields of wheat in the wind. I told myself the spume might be some quirk of the gale, an aberrant whirlwind plucking at the sea. But as the *Delaware* heaved on and the apparition came closer, I learned the spray marked the leaps of thousands of dolphins. Soon I could make out their graceful forms, curving like Greek statues on the glowing horizon, planting the fragile blossoms of their airborne moments each time they left and re-entered the green ocean. The school appeared without boundaries; it stretched from one end of the western horizon to the other. Every dolphin in the Atlantic must be here, I thought, overwhelmed by how little we know of the sea's true dimensions and the scope of the life it shelters.

It was that afternoon that recalibrated my attitudes, calmed me, cooled me, and made it possible for me at last to find the sleep from which someone pulls me with the urgency of his insistent voice.

"They shot Kennedy."

Even though I register the words, the ones that had been repeated over and over as I struggled to awaken, I do not comprehend. The deck hand sent to tell me must tell the story twice more. "Dallas . . . motorcade . . . Governor Connally . . . conspiracy . . . death . . ." the entire grim litany spills in the cabin darkness, and even when it ends, I cannot absorb the violence of the news.

"We're ordered back to port," the crewman tells me. "All government vessels are ordered in. We'll be home for Thanksgiving."

After two hours of trying to get through, I reach Jean on the radio-phone and tell her when to meet me at the Gloucester pier. Then I climb the steep steps to the dark wheelhouse where Joe sits slumped on his stool staring over the *Delaware*'s pitching bow and off across the implacable sea. I know I will not sleep this night.

141

Brunswick, Maine

March 4, 1986

Marty comes out of the darkness and rain into the light of our back stoop. He is carrying a package and his fine smile flashes from inside the drawn hood of his fisherman's slicker. Once in our kitchen, he drops the package on the counter and unwraps the damp, white butcher's paper and shows us the fresh halibut he is giving us.

"A noble fish," he says, and then laughs, white teeth bright against his lean-cheeked, weathered features. The halibut is about twelve pounds, caught that day, its brown, mottled hide still gleaming with its coat of fish oils, its eyes bright in its oddly shaped head.

"My favorite," I say. "There is nothing, nothing in this world, better than a fresh-caught halibut broiled by Jean." From across our kitchen Jean looks at the fish and at Marty, her eyes bright with the warmth of the moment on this raw and drizzly Maine March heartbreaker of a winter evening, come once too often as we wait for our shallow and deceitful spring.

But the halibut from our own waters is a certain signal

that the spring will come, and Martin Bartlett's exuberance after an entire day on the water is another. But then, he has always been charged with life and it is fine to have him visit, even if he cannot stay for dinner, will not taste his gift.

He is on his way to Rockland to see his lady. His boat, the *Penobscot Gulf,* is berthed in Portland and Marty will be aboard before first light tomorrow. He has little time.

A full-time commercial fisherman, he quit his work as a fisheries biologist quite a while back and bought the *Penobscot Gulf,* a steel-hulled sixty-footer that was built to haul coal from Boston to Maine-coast ports. Set flush in her main deck are the marine counterpart of steel manhole covers, round hatches screwed tight that open to hull compartments once used for coal. Marty has converted the design to a fishing vessel and fills the same compartments with ice on the way out, and hopes to have them filled with fish on the way home. He tried long-lining, using some of the knowledge he had absorbed aboard the *Delaware,* and now he makes day trips to the Gulf of Maine where he handlines for food fish.

Fresh halibut is his specialty and he sells to a selected group of stores and fine restaurants who want to be sure it's true when they say "fresh" on their seafood menus. The premium prices Marty gets for his premium products are just enough to keep him working at the life that gives him so much joy and independence.

"Sorry I have to leave so soon," he says, heading for the door, tugging at the fastenings of his slicker.

"So am I," I tell him. "You should stay for the feast."

Before he leaves, Marty stops and looks around our kitchen and at Jean and me. He doesn't say so, but I know he knows that each of us can still hear me shouting, "I love you" across the Atlantic and across twenty-three years.

Lake Clark, Alaska

July 11, 1986

T his is flying Alaska style: by sight, sound, and feel, "seat of the pants" navigation, a minimum of instruments and no high-tech navigational aids. From my window seat aboard the Twin Otter I can tell the two propellers are throttled back as far as safety will allow; any further drop in our rpms and the plane will be on the brink of stalling.

Our altitude cannot be more than a few hundred feet. Looking down at the dwindling waters of the Tlikakila River, I try to remember my Air Corps training. Once I knew how to judge altitude based on the size and scale of details on the ground. I've forgotten most of what I learned, but I know that if I can identify moose tracks across a sandy river bed that we are flying low—very low.

We can go no higher, not unless the pilot wants to enter the dimensionless and directionless void of the curdled rain clouds that press against the plane like the palm of some ghostly giant's amorphous hand, pushing with remorseless insistence ever closer to the valley's floor. I do not want to

145

think what will happen if we are forced out of the shrinking band of space we probe so carefully.

For this is, after all, true wilderness, almost three million acres of it, proclaimed so by the U.S. Department of the Interior, and we are bisecting its heart, making our way through Lake Clark Pass from Port Alsworth to the large, commercial airport at Anchorage, the one where we began this saga on the Fourth of July. From my window I can see only a small patch of riverbed, more sand, gravel, and bog than river during this relatively dry Alaskan summer—if Alaska's short span of long, gray, chill days can be called a summer. But I know there is more to be seen. If my vision could pierce the clouds and mist I might be even more tense than I am. For two of Alaska's most implacable glaciers rise from both sides of this ever-narrowing valley: Double Glacier to the east and Blockade Glacier just ahead to the north. The spectacle of these awesome masses of pearl and emerald ice took my breath away on the fifth, the day we flew into Lake Clark from Anchorage.

The sun shone that day, brilliant, high in its summer sky, and the plane that brought us through the pass banked along the glacier's edge, close enough for me to see the crushed, compressed wrinkles forced by millions of tons of moving ice. I looked up at mountain tops, not down, and that was when the flying weather was excellent. This forenoon, it is abysmal. This is a hazardous commute. There can be no question about the risk of this trip, a trip we surely would not be making if there were any alternative.

Planes get in trouble frequently in Alaska. There are reports of lost flights every week, every month. Yes, there are more planes per capita flying in this roadless state than any other, and, yes, the weather at this outer rim of the Arctic Circle is some of the most quixotic, most violent, and most unforgiving on the planet. And high-risk flying is the inevitable result of the combination. Today, I am certain all eight of the passengers aboard are asking themselves how they might fare if and when the Otter is forced down by the giant's implacable hand. If we survive the crash landing, if the pilot and co-pilot are lucky enough and skilled enough to ease the amphibian onto some accommodating bit of tundra, then what? We are coddled fishermen, not mountain rangers. This true wilderness under the glacier's great shadow demands survival skills and equipment we do not possess.

And yet, as the Otter literally picks its way through the pass, its throttles now at the absolute edge of control, props turning so slowly I think I can see the individual blades, we are each silent, grappling with the prospect of our own mortality in the endless halls of our imaginations and our memories. I hold Jean's hand and tell myself that as long as she and I are together all will be well, no matter what happens. I tell myself it is presumptuous to think so, but I am quite certain I have no fear of death. Seven years ago when my hepatic artery blew out and I was clinically "dead" for moments on the emergency operating table, I discovered death as a kind of biological and spiritual reality and was changed by that discovery.

There is nothing to fear, believe me. And I tell myself that on this risky flight and am calmed by it. But I also am hoping and wishing with as much kinetic energy as I can muster that the clouds will lift, that we will make it through the pass so Jean and I can live more of our lives together because we have so much fun doing it.

Unlike us, each of the other passengers is essentially alone and that, I think, must give their imaginations more room to roam. Solitude enhances anxieties, and as I glance around the cabin I quickly reconnoiter each face, playing a kind of game, to see what it reveals.

147

FISHING CAME FIRST

Bob Raphel is across the aisle. A Santa without his costume, he is an oversize man, tall, with ample flesh draped over his large bones, and the kind of happy belly that celebrates the good life. His expertise is finance, so I've been told, but his round, florid face with its ready, wide smile and blue eyes of enduring good humor never fit my steel-rimmed image of accountants and others who live with calculators in their pockets. I like to think Bob is thinking of his wife and children and their home in suburban Boston, but he's probably wondering what we could find to eat if we had to spend a few days in a glacier's shadow.

Much of Bob's recent professional life has been shared with another specialist, also in his mid-forties, who sits just in front of his co-worker. But Ed Faneuil's demeanor is quite the opposite: dour, slow to smile, the Boston attorney who specializes in real-estate negotiations gives nothing away. If he is pondering possibilities behind his closed eyes and gold-frame glasses, I have no way of knowing. Ed wears his negotiating personna through each day, whether or not he is at a conference table.

Both Bob and Ed have also spent countless hours with the third real-estate musketeer, Peter Mayer, a German-American who refuses to drop his starchy accent and who reads German-language newspapers almost every day. An engineer, Peter is still small, trim, and wiry in his early middle age because he works through almost all his waking hours, and he sleeps very little. Ruddy, sandy-haired, and literal, Peter is probably analyzing our speed, altitude, and course and trying to estimate our time of arrival at Anchorage. It seems to me to be the most probable way an engineer would react to our situation and Peter is an engineer by trait and trade if ever there was one.

Younger and less well defined than any of his three

148

professional associates, Ken Porter sits almost too far forward for me to be able to take any accurate reading of his mood. Unlike Peter, Ed, and Bob, Ken is not a cosmopolitan; he is still a country boy from a small Maine-coast town who is learning fast about the advantages of making a quick buck as a builder who invests in his own projects. From time to time, as we have met over the years in Maine, I have tried to find the message behind Ken Porter's remarkably wide blue eyes. As yet, I have discovered nothing but blueness and am certain this trip will end with no further revelations.

Scott LaBombard and his older brother occupy the two seats farthest forward, just aft of the cockpit bulkhead. In his mid-twenties, Scott is a fiercely impulsive young man still in transition from a tumultuous boyhood. Bravado is essential equipment in his daily survival kit, and Scott tries to keep defiance foremost among his attitudes. But most often I have sensed a formidable sadness instead. Yet even if I sat across from him, as his older brother does, I could not decipher Scott LaBombard's emotional code.

It is Pritam, that older brother, who launched us on this improbable Alaskan expedition and Pritam is so often airborne, has logged so many hours in so many airlines of so many nations in so many different kinds of aircraft that I am certain he has long since adopted a frequent flier's fatalism. If he senses any tension in the cockpit just in front of him, if he questions the need to fly just short of stalling speed two hundred feet above a glacial moonscape, he is not letting such matters intrude. If nothing else, his years of flying have taught him a kind of bored composure that is most useful on flights like ours.

It has cost him about $30,000 to take his four business associates, his brother, and Jean and me on this week-long fishing adventure in Alaska and what I wonder most as I

149

search his enigmatic expression is whether he had any fun. It is a difficult question to answer when it's asked about Pritam.

But for me, it's a breeze. Alaska's spectacle, the grandeur of the place, the discovery of wilderness fish, wilderness creatures, and breathtaking wilderness landscapes has been a constant joy, a succession of days of exploration and elation that put their indelible stamp on my consciousness. I lucked out again, and again it's fish that made me a winner. This trip began before our Iceland saga ended. Pritam discovered he and the Leirasveit's salmon were tuned to quite different frequencies: Pritam wanted fish that struck at every fly he cast; the distressed Atlantic salmon of that dry summer were too trapped to pay attention.

Miffed at the spectacle of hundreds of unhookable fish at his feet, Pritam spent an evening rehashing one of his favorite discussions: where to go in the world to find large fish in such numbers that contact between fish and fisherman could be all but guaranteed. The bluefish syndrome was still in force.

"Come on, John," he said, "there have got to be places where the fish come in herds. I see these photographs of guys standing beside piles of big, dead fish. I've seen pictures where the fish are bigger than the fishermen, fish with "2,000 pounds" painted on their sides hanging from racks with little, tiny fishermen standing there on the dock with their poles."

"Rods, Pritam, rods. Poles are what you use to catch catfish in a creek."

"Poles, rods, who cares. I want to go someplace where the fish are biting. I don't care how we catch 'em."

"Well," I said, thinking as much of my own opportunity as Pritam's, "I know there are plenty of fish in Alaska during the salmon runs. You must have seen the movies of

150

grizzly bears wading into a stream full of fish. They just put their heads underwater and come up with a mouthful of salmon. Those fish are so thick you can walk on their backs."

"Let's go there," said Pritam, his voice perking with the impulsive enthusiasm that is one of his most appealing traits.

Which was the start of the arrangements that may end with our forced landing on Double Glacier's ancient ice.

Two weeks after Iceland, I was having telephone conversations with a fellow named Chip Bates of Angler Adventures in Lyme, Connecticut. Shaw Mudge, who knows everyone in the fly-fishing world, gave me Chip's name, and it turned out to be a good one. Within a week of my first phone call, my desk in Brunswick was covered with Alaska fishing literature, most of it printed in four colors and all of it splattered with photographs of men, women, and children holding up an incredible collection of trophy fish: grayling, arctic char, rainbow trout, king salmon, and more. But it was an aerial shot that I knew would seal the deal for Pritam. Taken from above one of the many rivers of the Bristol Bay region, the photograph looks like an abstract painting—a swirling mass of blacks, grays, and the silver of the river. That's at first glance. Given more study, the dark mass at the center of the silver river becomes a school of salmon, a countless gathering that could satisfy even the most demanding prospect. If the fish come in such incredible numbers, the photograph says in very few words, then even you can catch some.

Before the first crocus bloomed beside our front door that February, Pritam signed with Chip and the trip that had been one of my life-long fishing-dream favorites was on its way to becoming reality.

Waiting at the private-plane runway of the Anchorage

airport on the morning of July 5th, I still had no clear notion of what to expect. I knew enough about four-color brochures to be certain Van Valin's Island Lodge might not be the paradise pictured. And I knew enough about the variables of fishing to know that while trophy fish might live in Lake Clark and its tributaries, catching them could be another story. And when the pilot of the Cessna that would take some of us to Port Alsworth stepped down from the plane and began loading our duffle bags, I began preparing my psyche for a letdown. He appeared to be no more than sixteen, and so short that he had to have a special cushion on his cockpit seat so he could see out the plane's windshield. But he brought us through Lake Clark Pass and past the Chigmit Mountain peaks as casually as he might take his girl downtown in the family car.

Glen Van Valin waited for us at Port Alsworth, a seven-house, one-airstrip settlement along the Lake Clark shore. The gravel strip's northeast end dipped to a ramp into the lake where Glen had parked his DeHavilland Beaver floatplane. After he loaded our baggage, Glen carried each of us on his back to the plane, helped strap us in, and took off for the island where he and his wife Sharon built their lodge fifteen years before, just ahead of new construction deadlines set by the National Park Service. When their lodge was finished, the Van Valins moved into the only fishing headquarters in this part of the world.

Their island, the lake, and the mountains around it are beautiful enough to take their place alongside any National Park panorama anywhere in the nation. When the deep greens and clear blues of the cold lake meet the lime forests of mountainsides that climb to peaks aglow with summer snow, they create what must be one of the most dramatic color contrasts in all of nature. And the entire sweep is unmarred by any witness to man. Only the lodge with its modest cabins on the island's eastern shore and the small ramp for float planes and boats are evidence of human visitors. All else proclaims that this is not home for man, but a place where hawks, bears, moose, fish, eagles, wolves, and mountain sheep can roam free to find their peace in a landscape all their own.

We are not prepared for this Alaska, Jean and I. Disappointed by Anchorage and its sloppy collection of franchise hotels, filling stations, and fast-food glitz, we hoped to discover the essential wild place of our imaginations. But now that we are here, we spend a good part of each day recalibrating our comprehension of a natural world. Nothing east or west of the Rockies has conditioned us for wilderness Alaska. There are no standards for comparison.

The closest I have come to Alaska's overwhelming wild space was on a 1943 training mission in the southwestern Arizona desert. Driven there in military trucks from the Army Air Corps gunnery school in Kingman, I spent two weeks firing real bullets from fifty-caliber machine guns. I practiced on the ground and in the air and that was the reason for our solitude. The Army was taking no chances with its clumsy beginners; we were sent to a place that was as far from any other place as any location in the country. But alongside Alaska, that distant corner of the desert was suburban. Flying above it at night, I could see the glow of Los Angeles lights in the west, and when I awakened in my bunk as the desert welcomed its silent and delicate dawn I sometimes heard trucks rumbling on a distant highway.

At Lake Clark, no roads curled within hearing distance. No city lights reflected in the night sky and in the primordial darkness stars moved as close as lamps in a window. The path from the dock to the lodge was the only path for hundreds of miles. Even if we had wanted to, we could not have walked out. And each morning when we taxied across the lake for our splashing float-plane takeoffs on our trips to rivers and lakes where Alaskan fish live, we flew for hours, low over land and water, and never saw a wisp of evidence to contradict the notion that we were the only human beings on the planet.

But we did see plenty of evidence that we had company. Moose lifted their bulbous noses and antlered heads as Glen banked his Beaver to give his passengers a better view. A fox trotted gracefully across a dun tundra and a grizzly mother ran alongside her cub, both of them loping along a streambed in the odd see-saw, rear-up/head-down/rear-down/head-up gait that is the grizzly cruising speed, designed, I like to think, to fool us into believing they can't move much faster.

Alaska is natural space in dimensions unknown to the hundreds of millions of Americans who have never been there—millions that included the eight of us until this Fourth of July. And because that space is so clearly beyond our experience, so difficult to reference, Jean and I spent most of our time trying to absorb it, learning to live with it without feeling the tremors that overtake travelers in a truly foreign land.

I cannot speak for the others, but I know that for Jean and me, fishing in Alaska was much more Alaska than fishing. The fish were there, of course. We took char from lakes, snagged chum salmon in coastal rivers, and, on a rafting trip down a winding, silver river bulging with clusters of emerald trout pools, Jean hooked, landed, and released an eleven-pound Alaskan rainbow more dramatically marked, more wildly beautiful than any trout in my memory. But Alaska overshadowed even that wonderfully complete episode.

Three days later, that rainbow's flush of tourmaline pink along its silver sides colors my memories. But I remember even more, and know I always shall, our meeting with Alaska a few minutes after the great trout had been set free. Jean, myself, Scott, and our guide sat high on the oversize tubing of the inflatable raft, our legs and feet meeting in the damp center circle of rubberized canvas that rippled underfoot whenever the raft scraped the watersmooth round rocks of the river bottom.

Scott sat opposite Bob, our young guide, and both held paddles used more for steering than propulsion. The river's natural current, softened by summer's rainless days, carried us gently at a pace calibrated to our enjoyment of that solitary landscape of tundra, brush, and mid-river islands of gravel topped with accumulated driftwood left by spring floods and their careening ice floes.

As we turned past a river bend, our raft revolving like a merry-go-round, the clear shoulder of a gravel bed pushed from the bank at the water's edge. As we watched, and as we moved closer, a large grizzly appeared in the brush just beyond the river bank, stepped down the slight incline, and stood on the open gravel slope, its broad and awesome head swinging directly at us, its dark eyes studying our progress with implacable curiosity and alertness. Every fiber of the bear's golden-brown presence spoke of the animal's supremacy. There was no hint of fear, no overtone of anxiety, not a shred of discernible surprise that the grizzly's search for massed salmon had brought it instead to a meeting with four humans in a rubber raft.

As the bear tipped its head and searched for our scent with its pitch-black nose, I kept telling myself to stay calm and, at the same time, another inner voice kept saying, "Jesus Christ! It's so big." I was well aware that we were in the presence of a creature who had every right to expect that we, not it, would give ground. Without a gun among us,

155

the four of us together did not have the collective strength the grizzly had in one tawny foreleg.

"I hope I don't see a cub next," Bob whispered and began paddling quietly but urgently downstream. But Scott, his Kodak swinging from his neck on its cord, paddled just as strenuously toward the bear. He wanted to get closer for a better snapshot of the first wild grizzly he had ever seen in camera range. With two well-conditioned young men paddling in opposing directions, the round raft began spinning in place, gathering speed as each paddler increased his tempo. Scott, more aggressive, more determined, seemed to me to be gaining. Spin as we might, we also made slow but persistent lateral progress toward the bear.

Absolutely aware of every inch of every change in our position, the grizzly appeared to be making a decision. Its eyes never left us, and its body pivoted slowly where it stood, keeping us in head-on view. Still implacable, the bear nevertheless began revealing a new, alert tension. I could sense from the movements of that monumentally broad head that the grizzly was deciding just how much closer we could come before we became invaders of its space. I did not want to learn the conclusion of that blunder.

"Scott!" I yelled. "Stop paddling!"

He stopped just long enough to look at me, his eyes questioning my illogical order.

"I want to take its picture," he said.

"No closer," I answered. "No closer. Let's get out of here. That's a wild grizzly and we're already too close."

My yelling had, for the moment, interrupted Scott's efforts. Meanwhile, Bob had redoubled his and as Scott and I kept up our stressed dialogue, Bob moved us away from the bear and out into a stronger current that carried the raft downstream at an accelerating clip.

Then the grizzly made its decision. Without a sound, it turned where it stood and loped unhurriedly up the bank and vanished in the brush. Every particle of its demeanor told us the bear had left because it had other, more important callings and not because it was in any way unsettled by our presence.

That episode, I'm certain, will stay with me more vividly and far longer than any of Alaska's fish—except for the grayling.

On a dun morning when soggy clouds draped the mountaintops, Jean and I and Bill Baechler flew with Glen to Twin Lakes, about thirty miles east-northeast of the lodge. Landing near the northernmost end of the northernmost of the two adjacent lakes, we waded ashore close to the mouth of the sturdy stream that is the lakes' parent. To the west, an impressive mountain rose against a sunless sky and when Glen took off he banked steeply, made one circle, waggled his wings, and was gone. The three of us were alone with only the clothes on our backs and the few supplies Bill had packed for our lunch. Watching the Beaver vanish in the clouds, I thought hard about the frailty of the human frame, about our dependence on the paraphernalia of so-called civilization, and about how sincerely I hoped no random occurrence would interfere with the promised return of the plane later that afternoon. We were, the two of us, totally dependent on Bill, not merely for our fishing, but our lives.

He was a guide well equipped to ease my anxieties. A friend of the Van Valins, he had spent the past fifteen summers at Lake Clark and most of his life in Alaska. He looked the part. Tall, broad, and bearded with gentle, brown eyes and a weathered visage, he wore a vintage cap, fly-fisherman's vest and packed a .44 Colt Magnum revolver in a leather holster strapped alongside his hunting knife. The

157

.44, he said, was the pistol most likely to give a grizzly pause.

Hiking east along the edge of the feeder stream, we were kept single file by the hefty brush and stunted evergreens that pressed close to the water's edge. Meeting a bear in this woody confine, I told myself, would be more than my constitution could stand: one ursine snort of surprise and my heart would stop. Well, at least I would be spared the agony of those taloned paws tearing my skimpy flesh from my delicate bones.

About a half-mile upstream, the woods backed off a bit and gave the stream a chance to broaden. Stopping, we sat on a moss bank while Bill chose a couple of gnat-sized flies and tied them to gossamer leaders. Looking at the stream, especially here where it flowed so thinly over a gravel delta, I could see no sign of fish. I told myself I could see any creature more than two inches long through this crystal water and I wondered if we were going to have to hike another half-mile to find what we had come so far to discover.

But this was the place. Handing us our rods, Bill told us to wade carefully and quietly to the center of the stream and cast from there so the small, wet fly quartered in the current. We did as we were told, and after the twenty minutes it took me to get accustomed to casting such light tackle in such limited space, my line tightened as a grayling struck. Splashing in the thin water, it ran upstream, shook its head, came downstream toward me, and then turned again. The fish never ran off enough line for me to use the reel. I worked the two-pound grayling with the flyline in my left hand while my right held the small rod high—the most intimate and subtle fishing that exists. Every motion of the fish communicates straight from the creature to the angler's fingers and from those fingers to his consciousness.

158

Lake Clark, Alaska ✦ *July 11, 1986*

Feeling the thumps, sensing the runs, anticipating a leap and, finally, acknowledging the fish's weariness, its resignation, there comes a moment of regret at the panic I have caused it and, at the same time, sadness that our meeting must end.

Together Jean and I hooked, landed, and released a half-dozen of the gleaming, pewter-hued grayling with their splendid dorsals unfolding like silken silver petals along their trim, dark backs. We lost more than we landed and within the hour the fish sensed our invasion of their wilderness home and paid no further attention to our flies, even though Bill tried several different patterns.

Following the stream back to the lake's edge, we waited there while Bill gathered firewood for the campfire that browned our hot dogs and heated our coffee. From that upper reach of the long lake, looking across the steely water at the mountainside rising so steeply on the opposite shore, I had even more of a sense of being small and quite alone in a vast and imposing country where what is wild rules. But Bill, who has learned not to dwell on isolation with guests who have seldom experienced it in such large doses, chattered his way through the meal and its restful aftermath.

Drowning the fire with lake water and walking a few steps into the tule and cattails, Bill surprised us when he emerged pushing a small, wooden skiff toward the water's edge.

"Dropped this in here from a Chinook helicopter," he explained. "This the last home port this boat will have."

He rowed us a hundred feet or so offshore and we used spinning rods and weighted lures to try to tempt some of the Arctic char Bill told us might be waiting in a deep hole. We drifted, feeling for the drop-off. Uncertain, I missed several strikes and handed my rod to Bill. On the next drift he boated a five-pound char that was one of the most dra-

159

matically colored fish I'd ever seen. Its dark-green back, highlighted by crimson spots, was contrasted by a vivid, terra-cotta belly and gill plates, ventral and anal fins rimmed with bands of bright, white trim. With additional splashes of white at its cheeks and jaws, the char looked as if it had been hand-painted for display over a saloon bar so customers could argue about whether it was a real fish or one a taxidermist invented.

We fished through the afternoon and Jean and I each hooked a small lake trout, but there were no more char. As the light began to fade from the low clouds that had followed us through the day, the lake began turning from steel to lead gray, and from gray to a shade of charcoal. I never once asked what time Glen was scheduled to fly in and take us home, but the question gained considerable weight in my thoughts as time crept by. When there were just moments left before the question could no longer be contained, I heard a plane's distant engine and in a few minutes looked up to see the Beaver circling.

"How was your day?" asked Glen as he helped me and Jean into the cabin's rear seats.

"Great," I answered, "just great. The best one of the trip."

We took off, banked, and circled for a last look. I had surprised myself when I told Glen the day had been our best. I hadn't made any judgments, done any balancing of one against the other. Reaching across the seat, I took Jean's hand in mine and looked into her gentle, brown eyes. Smiling, she looked back and told me without words that, yes, the day had been a fine one.

I am beginning to learn, at long last, I tell myself as I look down the aisle of the Otter at Pritam, that it is the quality of the total fishing experience that means the most, and not the number of fish caught and killed, their size and weight or the brute strength tested in any battle between fish and fisherman. We, Jean and I, traveled almost 4,000 miles to a remote Alaska stream to take a few, small grayling on light fly rods and it is this that will always bring us the warmest memories of our journey. It's one I never could have predicted, and one that makes me forget for a while that we are still, the eight of us and our pilot and co-pilot, just two hundred feet above the Tlikakila River.

If—no, *when*—we get home, I tell myself, I am going to become a better fly fisherman, a better fisherman all around. And, I decide, I will release the fish I hook, except one or two pan fish I may keep for a meal. I know mine is a fishing decision that has been made by tens of thousands of fishermen before me, but that doesn't stop me from feeling good about it. I want to tell each of the others on the plane, and especially Pritam, that they will find more pleasure in their trips if they stop being so concerned about how many fish they catch, and start thinking about how well they make contact with each of the fish they meet, small, large, common, or rare. These meetings, I tell myself, must be as intimate as possible. Every fish, like our grayling on those fly rods, must be allowed to speak in its loudest and clearest voice and must be listened to attentively. This means using the most appropriate and sensitive tackle and making certain the meeting does not permanently damage the fish that gives so much.

Nor should it permanently damage us fishermen, I tell myself, looking down at a merciless wedge of glacial ice. As I do, the sound of the Otter's engines grows louder, the rpms increase, the plane lunges forward.

Here we go, I tell myself, knuckles pale as pearls as I grip my seat's armrests.

Sudden sunshine floods the passenger cabin, sunshine as

bright as the snow I can see on the mountain peaks from my window. I can see! That realization is so joyous I don't try to explain the surreal Alaska weather that has us flying all but blind one minute and the next showers us with sun from a cloudless sky.

The Otter is climbing now, as if it, too, cannot quell its exuberance at its new freedom. I look down at the dancing waters of Cook Inlet and know that we will follow them to Anchorage just up the bay.

Key West

February 13, 1987

Roger is here, beside me on the Mako's only passenger seat in front of the stand-up console. Jeffrey is at the controls behind the console and has the Yamaha outboard cranked up. It is one of those fine midwinter mornings in this place of climatic blessings so generous I am still unable to accept them without comment.

"What a morning!" I yell into Roger's nearby ear. "Wow, what a morning." And I give him a solid poke with my elbow to make certain he gets my message.

Aside from the slightest of nods, he does not respond. I tell myself he does not want to exert nonessential energy shouting over the motor's roar, but I know better. Roger has spent each of his thirty-four years perfecting the art of cool. He is not about to let any enthusiasm, even the boundless joy a Maine Yankee can find in a seventy-eight-degree February morning, overtake his determination to maintain a stolid visage. He will stifle any tremor that might become a smile, inhibit any zest that might invigorate his few words, and maintain his "I've-seen-it-all-before" demeanor no matter how outlandish the happenings born before his steady blue eyes and the contact lenses that make them seem even more removed.

Keeping the essential cool is Roger's armor and he has much to protect. Unleashed, the very emotions that could welcome this elegant morning might also sweep him into his past. Rather than run the risk of dealing with a personal history of emotional extremes, Roger shuts down every valve and moves through his days with every shadow closeted, every flue effectively damped.

Fishing excites and pleases him; I know this, but only because I have known Roger for some twenty years and, with Jean's help, have learned a little about how to understand him. Our son Bob brought Roger home for supper one autumn evening. They were junior high school classmates and each of our sons seemed able to persuade at least one of his classmates to stop by our house for a meal almost every school day and some weekends. I paid as little attention as possible. The burden, after all, was Jean's. It was she who had to cook and serve the extra meals. She had eight family mouths to feed on any given day. I reasoned that one or two or three more, once we got past a half-dozen, made little difference.

However, after a week of seeing Roger's world-weary face across the dinner table I took Bob aside and asked casually how long his guest might be staying. When Bob's reply seemed charmingly evasive, I resolved to press the matter with Jean. When it came to household dynamics, she knew everything, including everything our sons and daughters thought they were keeping secret.

"What's with this guy Roger?" I inquired when, at long last, we were alone with midnight's silence.

"He's gentle, isn't he?" Jean answered. "He's so quiet so much of time I hardly notice him."

So much for answering my question.

I pressed on and finally Jean told me she thought Roger might not have another home to go to. When I pressed further I got a brief narrative of family traumas within Roger's own world. And I got the news that his stay might easily be indefinite.

Five years later, I was still wondering how long Roger would be getting his mail at our address. And five years after that, I was still wondering. Not that Roger had been at our house the entire time. He made trips here and there: Montreal, Kansas City, Miami, Key West, Manhattan, Boston, New Delhi . . . wherever his whims and wanderlust might take him. But even if those travels landed him in Katmandu, which they did, he would, eventually, return and begin giving our phone number to friends who might want to reach him.

When romance, so long postponed, entered his life he left us and began housekeeping with his fine lady. But even that happy arrangement, which seemed so solid, did not last. Indeed, the breakup came shortly after Jean and I arrived in Key West for this, our first winter away from Maine since we were married there decades ago. We had been here something less than three months when we came downstairs one morning and found Roger asleep on our sofa.

Always susceptible to a kind of languid despondence, Roger, when he awakened, seem more depressed than usual. The breakup was taking its toll. In twenty years I had learned that nothing I could say, not even a quote from Norman Vincent Peale, could alter the course Roger had set for himself through the slough of despond. But events, I had also learned, could speak louder than words. Roger loves fishing, I told myself, and he especially loves fishing when he catches fish better and faster than you.

One of the few moments when Roger's cool blew was after he and Bob had taken the dory onto Middle Bay to fish for striped bass. I told them where the fish might be,

165

and said I also intended to fish the same spot from the Whaler. When I got there, I could see the dory across the cove about a mile away. Well, I told myself, those boys know what I meant and they can see me. If they have any brains they'll soon be over here where the fish are.

After an hour or so of casting into the best part of the falling tide I accepted the fact that the fish had not made their swing through my hot spot. It happens. I quit and headed home. As I made the Whaler fast to her mooring, I heard a shout from the dock, looked up, and saw Roger holding up about a four-pound striper.

"Where were you?" he called, and began laughing, bent over laughing. I could not decide if I should be chagrined at my defeat, or elated at Roger's victory and the joy it gave him.

I never forgot that joy and how much he loves fishing. Which is why, despondent as he may now be, he is beside me this morning as Jeffrey speeds out of Key West Harbor into the Gulf.

Our mission is well defined: we are looking for permit.

A great many anglers have spent a great many hours on South Florida's flats looking for permit. It is a search that sometimes takes them to exotic places like Belize where permit, so I've been told, swim in parading schools that arrive as regularly as notices from the Internal Revenue Service.

Here in the waters off Key West in February no such inevitability exists. Permit, a staple of the reef population a generation ago, have, like so many other once-abundant species, become scarce. Unable to withstand the familiar twin pressures of overfishing and the degradation of their habitat, the odd, awesome and quite mysterious fish have attained a kind of nobility in sportfishing lexicons. Some of the current reverence for permit relates to their increasing rarity, but the fish also has its personna going for it.

166

A permit is large, wary, lovely, elusive, and is the Hulk Hogan of the fish universe. Hooked, a permit fights as doggedly, as strenuously, and as intelligently as any creature in the sea. And they are well equipped for their work. Not counting blowfish and other blobby spheroids, and leaving out the flatties—rays, skates, halibut and fluke and flounder—there are two basic fish families: the torpedos and the dinner plates. Torpedos are the best known because they are the stereotypical fish: essentially cylindrical bodies tapered at both ends rather like a cigar, mouth and teeth at one end, forked tail at the other. Striped bass, bluefish, barracuda, tarpon, bonefish, salmon, trout, guppies, and tens of thousand of other are torpedos. Less abundant, but almost as well known, the dinner-plate family includes scup, perch, pompano, lookdowns, and permit, to name just a few. These fish swim like a dinner plate on edge. Indeed, some are so symmetrically shaped that they are almost perfectly round. They have larger eyes in relation to their size than most torpedoes, and, when they swim upside down, as I have seen some dinner plates do, it is difficult for a casual observer to tell the difference. The top half looks the same as the bottom half, and vice-versa.

The permit is the dinner platter of the dinner-plate tribe. It's bigger, smarter, heftier, stronger, tougher, and stubborner. There are, I'm certain, permit weighing sixty pounds swimming with the slow grace of all overweight beings around a coral reef within a few miles of Key West. Those fish could be four feet across from the top of their back to the bottom of their silver belly and about five feet from the push of their truculent jaws to the fork of their wide and wonderful scimitar tails.

I don't know anyone I could call a permit. We all know sharks and barracudas. I could name a few mackerel, one or two tarpon. But no one I would call a permit. The person would be large, quiet, shy, handsome, mysterious, well dressed, Republican, mature, reclusive, vital, shining, strong enough to bench press a thousand-pound barbell as if it were an empty laundry basket, and bright enough to finish *The New York Times* Sunday crossword puzzle in fifteen minutes or less.

In the lucid waters of the flats southwest of Key West, a swimming permit, if you are lucky enough to see one, looks like a mass of silver and blued gun metal, an amorphous shape rather than a defined presence, a mercurial shadow navigating a coral reef or a marl flat as deliberately and shyly as a Union League Club member on his way to a bridge game when he is supposed to be heading home to dinner. Every so often, in truly thin water, permit will become so enchanted by their own skills at pushing crabs out of the marl with their pugnacious jaws that their scimitar tails wave like slim, dark blades taking swipes at the sky. Guides who pole their flats skiffs as skillfully as Jeffrey can sometimes get within casting range of tailing permit, but not often. Permit seem to know when every skiff leaves the dock and they do not linger to learn if it's headed for them.

We will not see permit tailing on this fragrant, satin morning that has given us the Gulf as flat as a cornflower table cloth spread for us alone. Jeffrey has discovered a permit lounge on a corner of an otherwise unremarkable stretch of coral and marl at the edge of a flat crossed by scores of boats each pleasant Key West day. I never asked Jeffrey how he found the place; he made me swear never to reveal its location the first day we visited the spot and I have kept my pledge.

Whatever the attraction, the small—no more than a few hundred square feet—pocket lagoon and its six to eight feet of water just where the flat ends and tails off has become the latest restaurant on the permit "in" list. During the past three weeks on his cautious visits, Jeffrey has seen permit almost every day the weather allowed him enough underwater light. Neither he, nor anyone, knows what has brought the fish from their dark depths to this modest locale. But whenever the tide and wind are right, a clubby group of a dozen or more permit gather to graze around the single, large coral rock that is their center table.

Jeffrey is scanning his ranges and the submerged signposts that only he can read as he tries to put Roger within casting range. Roger, with his light spinning rod at the ready, stands attentive, but cool, on the Mako's flat bow deck. He has never seen a permit, does not know what he is looking for, but will respond to whatever instructions Jeffrey gives.

I have made previous visits. The most recent, about two weeks ago, was an unforgettable and traumatic encounter, the sort that can destroy a relationship.

Like Roger, I stood on the *Waterlight*'s bow, spinning rod at the ready. About ten feet of line had been stripped from the reel and dropped into the water where it trailed as Jeffrey poled from his stern platform. A single, keen steel hook was fast to the end of the eight-pound-test monofilament and there with the hook's point worked up through the tough outer rim of its shell was an olive-drab crab about the size of a silver dollar and almost as round. I kept the crab in the water because it needed to be alive and sprightly, just the sort of snack a cruising permit might find impossible to resist.

I was not too encouraged by the odds. On several previous trips I had cast crabs that were even more appetizing and watched as permit fled as soon as my offering dapped the surface. Either that or they approached, studied my deception with a large, intelligent, all-seeing eye, and turned away, their motion charged with scorn. Was I, the fish appeared to be asking, stupid enough to believe a permit would eat a crab with a hook through its shell?

Permit fishermen, any fishermen for that matter, do not ponder such questions too strenuously. Such tendrils of doubt about the comparative intelligence of the creature in the boat and the one in the water can lead to lost confidence on the boat and that is the beginning of the end of a fishing day. A good fisherman, like every other athlete of accomplishment, must approach each contest with a full measure of assurance in his abilities.

Jeffrey knows this and spends as much time building his angler's confidence as he does finding fish and navigating his boat. From his poling platform he scans the surface of the Gulf and the surface of his fisherman with equal intensity. "Keep your crab in the water . . . Don't look directly into the glare . . . Remind yourself where to look when I say two o'clock or ten o'clock. I notice that sometimes you seem confused . . . When you can't see a fish underwater that I tell you is there, try moving your line of sight back and forth across the surface. Don't let your eyes focus on one spot and hold there . . ." The voice is calm, the attitude positive, helpful, and gentle. Never critical, even at moments of crisis.

"There's a fish, a good one, at ten o'clock, there, just off the coral head. Can you see him?" That was the way our saga began. I raised the rod tip, lifted the crab from the water, flipped the bail and cocked my arm ready to fire. But I did not see the fish. I thought I could, but then I always think I can, I am so anxious. I did see the "rock," as we have named this particular coral head that centers our permit grazing ground.

"He's to the right of the rock," Jeffrey called, his tone more electric. "He's a big fish. Can you see the rock?" He got as close as he ever has to letting impatience loose.

"Yes."

"Well cast to the right of the rock. That's good. That's good. He sees the crab. He's turning. Keep the crab moving. Don't let it sink in the grass.

"That's it. That's it. He's coming for it.

170

"He's going to eat it.

"There! There! He's got it.

"Strike him. Strike him."

I lifted the rod tip, leaned back and pulled my right hand and the rod sharply toward my shoulder. Then I felt resistance but no sense of life at the other end of the line.

"I think it's snagged in the weeds."

"No," Jeffrey yelled, "strike him again."

I reeled in a foot or two of line and when it tightened I pulled back hard. Again, the rod and line reacted as if my hook was imbedded in an old piling, or wedged in a coral crevice.

But the rock began to move, at first as if some underwater foot had given it a kick and sent it slowly down a submerged incline. Line left my reel as steadily as if it were tied to a truck geared to travel at precisely two miles an hour. Only one response was possible: I held the rod at close to a ninety-degree angle and let the rock roll as it pleased. My heart had begun to pound because I had come to comprehend that it was a permit, not a rock, at the far end of my line.

"It's a big fish," Jeffrey said, "big enough to run that line off the reel." He pressed the button on the electric motor that lowered the outboard's propellor just below the water line. "I may have to start up and follow that fish," he called.

I nodded okay. I felt a little dumb, standing there with nothing to do except watch the reel spool turn and listen to the low hum of the line under tension. I began to comprehend that I was in for a long morning on the bow.

"How much line left?" Jeffrey asked.

"Not much," was the best I could do. "I can see most of the sides of the spool."

"Okay," Jeffrey said. "I'm starting up."

When the motor caught, Jeffrey idled in neutral for a

moment, then eased into gear. We began following our fish, slowly and carefully.

"See if you can gain on him," Jeffrey told me, and I began regaining line, a few feet at a time.

Together the fish and I followed that routine for an hour. Then I began making some progress. Pumping, lifting the rod slowly until it was pointing at the sky and then dropping quickly and reeling as I did, I could hold the fish and, bit by bit, bring it closer.

Jeffrey had stopped using the motor, jammed his pole into the marl and made fast to it with a short length of line tied to one of the braces of his poling platform. "Staked off" is the flat guide's term for it.

No longer busy maneuvering the *Waterlight,* he could focus on buoying my spirits and overseeing my technique.

"You're doing a great job, John. Just a great job." Jeffrey said so with such enthusiasm and conviction that I believed him.

"He's a big fish. A record fish. A world's record." I had still to get my first look, and I accepted Jeffrey's opinion, but with reservations. I was sure he was trying to encourage me more than he was trying to gauge the permit's personal dimensions. But the adrenalin pulsed and I hung on.

After another half-hour I began to believe I could land the permit. Its runs had become progressively shorter and its stubborn standoffs when neither of us could move had become less frequent. Jeffrey had moved forward and stood right behind me, waiting for the fish to show, waiting for the double leader to break the water's surface.

"Keep him coming," he said. "I know you're tired, but keep him coming."

I was doing just that and I had the fish as close as it had been all morning—close enough for it to see the boat. During that phase of the struggle, the line holding the boat in place worked its way loose from the stake and we began drifting.

"Don't worry," Jeffrey said. "Concentrate on landing this fish. We can get the pole anytime."

When the permit got its look at the *Waterlight,* it began another headlong surge that took it in a straight line directly off the bow, then a long curve that became a 180-degree turn. Before either Jeffrey or I realized what was happening, the permit had passed the pole stuck in the marl and my line was being dragged along the pole's surface.

The fish kept going, pulling harder now across the pole so the line began inching up the pole's slope, getting closer and closer to the spreader at the end that was used to gain purchase on soft bottoms.

Jeffrey knew what might happen long before I did and he jumped overboard and began half-swimming and half-running toward the pole. He was almost there when the line reached the spreader, caught, stretched one last time, and broke.

Jeffrey slumped in the water and then began cursing. He blamed himself for the accident. I blamed no one. Instead, I was somehow content with the entire drama. That fine fish, I told myself, deserves its freedom. I said as much to Jeffrey.

But for the first time in the months that I'd known him and fished with him, he lost his temper. His face flushed, his mustache seemed to bristle straight out, his cheeks swelled and the blue eyes that so often flashed with glee now gathered their own flaming intensity. As he clambered back over the gunwale, water and mud dripping from his tanned legs, he spouted a stream of profanities and obscenities that I should have recorded for my files. He was, of course, angry at himself, utterly and completely chagrined and shamed by what he considered his lapse of judgment under stress. In Jeffrey's view, as skipper of the *Waterlight* and a professional fishing guide, the thought that one of his anglers should lose a possible world-record fish because the guide had made a mistake was more than his weary psyche could stand, especially after more than ninety minutes of combat maneuvers that had taken us across almost a square mile of that sapphire battlefield.

Slumped at the console, Jeffrey punched the starter button, sweat and sea water still dripping from his torso. "We're going in," he shouted. I kept my silence, studying the details of the reel in my hand. I wanted to tell Jeffrey to relax, to remember the wonderful intensity of the episode and not the events that had helped the fish find its freedom. But it was time for me to say nothing, and I worked at it.

The melodrama has not been mentioned this morning and I am hoping it will not be. Looking at the patchwork of wild keys and mangrove hummocks slumbering like great green cats curled against an azure horizon, watching the panorama of the sea floor unfold its browns, greens, blues, yellows, and bleached whites as we fly above it on our seawater sky, and feeling my spirits take wing as effortlessly as the man o'war birds gliding dark against luminous cumulus, I want no past, only this present, no other mornings, only this one. Incredible, I tell myself as I look off our stern quarter and see the bleached squares of buildings and spidery radio towers rising from Key West's southwestern shores. Here we are in a wilderness as pure as any moonscape and yet when our motor shuts down the northeast breeze will bring us the sound of heavy machinery at work on the Truman Annex concrete piers.

This is the Key West secret, this nearness of true paradise to the place that's sold as paradise but is honky tonk at heart. Once on the water, once on the flats, once suspended above this world ruled by tides, creatures, and the mystery of the universe, we are adventurers in a wilderness garden. Like the proverbial fly in amber, we are suspended in the clarity of time, space, and these languid waters that caress all those who inhabit them. Such voyages are better taken each in their own setting; those of the past should be left behind; those of the future should be left alone.

Jeffrey seems to agree. His spirits are up. As he poles slowly across the flats, he chatters of today. "Keep your eyes from looking into the glare, Roger . . . Be sure to cast when I tell you, even if you don't see the fish . . . It's a great morning for fishing . . . Don't fall asleep up there."

Roger is in his coolest mode: shoulders slumped, face expressionless, eyes focused on some distant and mystic event only he can perceive.

But he is quite aware of his whereabouts. When Jeffrey gets down to business, Roger is wide awake.

"Permit at two o'clock," Jeffrey calls. "About one hundred feet out. More than one fish. They're out of range, but get ready.

"Okay, Roger. Can you see the fish? Two of them, moving from two o'clock to twelve o'clock, right off the bow."

Roger does not reply. He has yet to see the fish, but does not want to admit it. Instead, he nods.

Jeffrey, tolerant, calls out, "Cast now, cast to twelve o'clock, straight ahead."

Roger learned his casting in Maine and is a well-coordinated and strong young man. Only his attitude is out of shape. His cast is a long one and the crab touches down lightly.

"Reel in. Reel in," Jeffrey says. "They are moving left. Cast again to ten o'clock, more to the left."

175

And Roger does. He retrieves his crab slowly, steadily, just as Jeffrey instructed.

"He's going to eat it," yells Jeffrey.

Roger's rod bends. He strikes the fish and there is instant ferocity at the other end. Line hums off the reel.

"Holy shit," says Roger, "he's really bookin' it."

Jeffrey stakes off, stands at Roger's side and feeds him constant messages of encouragement and instruction. In a half-hour, an eighteen-pound permit is alongside ready to be released, but not before it is weighed and held up proudly by Roger as he poses for his photograph with his trophy and one of the widest smiles he has worn in a month of Sundays.

"Now it's John's turn," Jeffrey says, and we begin another prowl. He does not say so, but I know he is thinking that the odds are against hooking two permit on the same morning in the same location. He presses his search, thinking now with me on the bow with the same rod in my hand of the drama here two weeks ago and hoping that this time neither of us makes a mistake.

We don't.

Within twenty minutes, I am fast to a big permit. Just seventy minutes later I am striking the same pose Roger was. But my permit weighs thirty-four pounds and I am so pleasantly spent from the fight that Roger has to hold it while Jeffrey takes our photograph.

This time, both of us are smiling wide, long smiles. So is Jeffrey. All of us have forgotten past errors and are swept away by present success.

When it is released, the big permit lumbers off reminding itself not to eat any more crabs with hooks through their shells.

The Marquesas

February 29, 1988

T̲he Marquesas Keys are a wonderful mystery. Some Key West historians will tell you the ring of small islands about twenty-five miles southwest of Key West is the only atoll in the Atlantic. I have never been to the islands of the Pacific, but I have seen enough aerial photographs of atolls to know that they mark the graves of long ago volcanos or mountains that sank beneath the sea. A lagoon shimmers at the center of a round, geologic crown of rock and coral: all that's left of the rim of an ancient volcanic peak.

The Marquesas, the popular argument goes, are the remnants of just such a prehistoric drama, a geologic anomaly that rose from the primeval sea far from its brethren in what is now Mexico. Other folks have other thoughts about the unique formation that marks the end of the necklace of keys and hummocks draped along the meeting ground of the Atlantic and the Gulf from Key West to the Tortugas. Some reason that the ring of coral sand and marl was formed in an earthquake. "Mexico is not that far off," they

177

say, "and earthquakes have been happening there for centuries."

Knowing nothing of geology, and less about the genesis of the Marquesas, I can believe the theory I like best. And there is one. Jeffrey tells me there are informed Keys mariners who believe the Marquesas are the child of a meteor—some giant fragment of infinity that plummeted from outer space, or perhaps from another universe. So far removed in time that its fiery flight went unmarked by any being, the visitor from the unknown hurled itself into the warm salt seas of the shoals that rise on the western rim of the Boca Grande Channel. Blazing, hissing, smashing into its final grave, the meteor's calamity left its own mile-wide mark on the sea floor, an almost perfectly round depression wreathed by a circle of islands and hummocks forced from the center of the meteor's impact just as mud squeezes from around a boot sole pressed into a puddle.

Tended by a milennia of solitude, the raw material pushed from the sea bottom acquired its dry-land biota. First the tiny plants that are children of wind-blown seeds, then the mangroves, propagated by currents and sea-bird droppings. And finally the maturing greenery that is south of Florida's horticultural signature: impenetrable tangles of mangrove roots, scrub pine, sawgrass, and dozens more species and sub-species of green, growing vegetation that defies human perambulation and appears consummately designed to protect every anonymous marl hillock from the kind of heedless human exploration that's so often memorialized by the extinction of the very places that once held mystery in their grasp.

Bulldozers, of course, can make an instant mockery of mangroves. In moments, lowered blades eradicate the work of eons, sparing nothing, not even the only salt-sea memento of a dying meteor's final flight. That could have happened, probably would have happened if the Marquesas and their sister keys to the north had not been protected by the Department of the Interior, which has recently stamped "National Wildlife Refuge" across every map of the watery territory that stretches from Fort Taylor at the end of Key West's Southard Street to Fort Jefferson in the Tortugas. I am no fan of the Federal bureaucracy, but each time I look southwest from any Key West vantage point, and every time I navigate those azure waters in any sort of craft I write a silent note of gratitude to Nat Reed and everyone else in Interior's Washington labyrinth who engineered the decisions and agreements that have become such an effective shield for what is, I'm certain, the globe's largest submerged national park and wildlife refuge. There is, on Woman Key's northeast corner, witness to what might have happened if Interior had not acted. Not that David Wolkowsky built himself an ugly retreat; he did not. His elevated, wood-framed and wood-sheathed house at the edge of a crescent of pure white beach is a graceful and sensitively sited structure: the only one between Key West and the Marquesas, built before the territory was taken out of public circulation. But each time I pass it, it shouts to me of a future these keys might have known.

We will not hear its voice today. We are, Jean and I and Jeffrey, aboard his *Waterlight* on a course through the Lakes, the interlocked stretch of shoal channels on the north side of the line of keys that follow the reef from Key West to Boca Grande Key at the northern rim of Boca Grande Channel. David's house faces south, and besides, we are a mile or more north of Woman Key racing across turtle grass flats in water so clear and so smooth I can see individual blades of grass waving in the current.

How lucky I am. When I made this date with Jeffrey a week ago, there was no way of knowing what our weather would be. Like February everywhere, the month in Key West arrives with surprises. One dawn will open the curtains on a dark melodrama acted by rolling clouds stuffed with rain and thunder. Others torment the sea and land with winds like those that pushed Jeffrey and me into the lee of Archer Key just three days ago. I have been remembering that day and more as I waited for this one.

Because this one was memorable even before it arrived. I had Jean's promise that she would come with me to the Marquesas, the scene of adventures that come to a fisherman only if he is blessed by the fates—adventures that are as vivid in my history as any I have lived. Each has been narrated to Jean in detail, each has been retold to others as Jean listened, wondering I'm sure how many times a tale can survive retelling. This two-week visit to Key West would not go by, I promised myself, without a trip to the Marquesas with Jean.

But only if the weather is right: that was an addendum to my pledge. Jean is not a complainer; she would have made the trip in any weather Jeffrey considered navigable. But I know she is a creature of the land, not a spirit of the sea. She endures every discomfort in the service of her garden; she will politely refuse almost every invitation that involves leaving port.

But given this day's splendor, even an earth mother is exhilarated by the sea. We are afloat on a shimmering mirror of a cloudless sky. At thirty knots, the *Waterlight* glides like raw silk pulled across a polished table. Today, earth's reassuring firmness reaches to encompass a sea as smooth as a meadow in May. Jean's soul rests content.

Over the decades of my wage-earning work as a journalist I would, in times of particular drudgery, push away from my desk and confide to my co-workers that I was on the brink of abandoning not only my job but my home community and my entire life's routine. Asked what I would do and where I would go I would say with considerable conviction that I would start over on some island in the Carribbean set at the center of the finest fishing waters on the planet. "I will," I told my listeners, "spend my days in a small boat afloat on a crystal sea where fish flash bright greetings under a tropic sun."

"Yes, that sounds fine," those skeptics would reply, "but how long do you think you can do that before you get bored."

And my answer was always the same. "I'll try it for twenty-five years, and then take a second look."

Each time I told that ritualized tale, I saw myself at the center of a shoal-water universe, alone with my fish and my fishing. Soon the fancy became a dream, a dream I began to want desperately to come alive.

And today, I tell myself, it has. And today, I tell myself, I know what I said is true: I can do this for the rest of my life, however long or short it may be, and be truly happy doing it. And happiest when Jean and Jeffrey are with me.

When we reach Boca Grande Key and make the turn that starts us across Boca Grande Channel, I am now and at last positively certain of this day's mercies and splendors. The region's entrance to the Gulf of Mexico from the Straits of Florida and the southern Atlantic, this channel is like so many places where two headstrong waters meet. Even on windless days, the surface surges with restless tides and currents ebbing and flowing across Boca Grande Channel's four miles. Pushing two seas together in such relatively narrow confines and in such relatively shoal water is a process sure to encounter resistance. With no room to run, the two seas meet here in an endless turbulence that roils even windless waters. And when gales do blow, this is not an easy place to be. Odd-shaped swells approach from nowhere, rolling against wind and tide; even the most seaworthy boat and experienced helmsman cannot avoid a pounding. I have made the crossing several times with Jeffrey when the best I could do was hold on, grit my teeth, and pray that we would soon reach sheltered waters.

And while I prayed, I tried not to remember that the world's record hammerhead shark was taken from these very waters, a great and terrifying fish almost twenty feet long weighing more than a ton. There are others down there in the depths, I am certain, as massive as the meteor that's buried somewhere beneath the bottom of the Marquesas lagoon.

Today the channel is so wonderfully benign that as we cross I inform Jean of its hammerhead distinction. That's how certain I am of this day's good fortune.

Given my Marquesas history, I should be more restrained. On other fine days, other orchid mornings, I have cruised this same course across a well-mannered channel, my hopes flying like a banner in the dawn. Yet those very days kept a secret from me, a shock they delivered just as I began to believe I held paradise in my grasp.

Ten months ago four of us crossed Boca Grande on an early May morning as soft as a newborn kitten. Jeffrey, my brother-in-law John Graves, his wife, my sister Jane, and myself. Jeffrey seldom carries more than two fishermen; as he does so often, he gave me his blessing and made room. In return, I promised that John and Jane would do the fishing; it was, after all, their charter.

We were looking for tarpon, and Jeffrey brought us to the right place. The reefs, islands, hummocks, and dunes that define the Marquesas lagoon are not a perfect circle. The curving half-circle of land on the northeast quadrant is the largest single land mass: a single, sheltering arm that protects the lagoon from the northeast winds that prevail. To the southwest, its counterpart land arc is a series of small, and even smaller islands and hummocks. Both Gulf and Atlantic tides and currents sweep along the channels between these independent mangrove masses. Like arteries, the channels feed the shallow lagoon, circulating nourishing sea water across the mile-wide flats. Of these channels, the entrance to the largest is on the due-south curve of the Marquesas circle. Here where its entrance waters are almost ten feet deep, is one of the places where migrating tarpon move on their journey from the dark depths of the ocean to their shoal spawning grounds off the southern coast of Mexico.

Certainly not I, nor any of the fishing people I have spoken with, can come up with a dependable reason why tens of thousands of these huge and graceful silver fish should choose to navigate this single, small channel on their thousand-mile voyage to their mating and nursery destinations.

Look at the chart. A few miles southwest of the Marquesas, just beyond the Quicksand Shoals, there is a channel ten miles wide and more than a hundred feet deep that reaches all the way to the Dry Tortugas. Why haven't the tarpon made that their central passage? There they could find invisibility in the depths; here at the Marquesas, their wonderfully prehistoric, deep-sided, armor-scaled massive shapes glide like shimmering projectiles across the white sand of the channel mouth in water so stunningly clear I have, I swear, seen my reflection in a tarpon's dark globe of an eye as the fish soared under our bow.

I think John Graves is a year or so older than I. Because I've never asked, I do not know. I can, however, vouch for his gristle. A Marine lieutenant who fought and lost an eye in World War II, he is a Texas man in every sense of the weight that heaviest of states implies. His parents and grandparents are the same and John has written some of the finest, and it is so acknowledged, Texas history, Texas prose, and Texas anecdote that can be found in any library of contemporary history and literature. Unlike me, he is a scholar, albeit one who lives on a two-bit ranch he made for himself in a tiny town called Glen Rose a few miles southwest of Fort Worth.

Because he is a scholar, and because he has, in the latter years of his active outdoor life, taken on fly fishing as his mission, he was especially enchanted by the prospect of casting one of his hand-tied flies to the largest and most spectacular fighting fish a fly-caster can find. A husky, weathered man who looks like the rancher he also is, John makes his own fly rods on Sage blanks, mounting each guide and applying each coat of lacquer with as much patience as he gives to the individual well being of the cattle and the goats that are so superbly cared for in Glen Rose.

I have always been fond of John, primarily because we got off to a fine start. Before he married my sister Jane some thirty-five years ago, she was a New York City debutante, a properly educated young lady whose college years had cost the family a bundle. She knew a great many old-money sons and daughters and, I'm certain, Helen, our mother, harbored high hopes that Jane would, in Helen's words, "Marry well." Honestly defined, the phrase meant marrying old money.

Well, in Texas John Graves might be considered old money, but Texas is a young state and I'm certain my mother never had in mind a man who wore blue jeans to restaurants and hopped in his pickup truck with cow flop on his stable boots. Nor did she think that the best Jane could do would be to hook up with a man who planned on building his own house, limestone block by limestone block in a far corner of a state famous for its far corners. "But nobody knows him!" Helen often said; or "Who does he know?" John, as it turned out, had many close and distinguished friends when he met Jane, but, as Helen said, "They're no one we know, dear."

So I was anxious to see how the first encounters would develop when John arrived in New York for the wedding. He was, I had been advised, not a party man. Indeed, the odds were high, a mutual friend advised me, that John Graves would not appear at any of the various receptions and dinners that preceded the ceremony. But he did, and he won. He somehow made it clear by his demeanor and actions that while he obviously believed the city social scene to be something less than bullshit, he would, nevertheless, do what was proper and courteous on Jane's behalf.

He appeared at the gatherings, but he kept himself at a polite Texas remove. Helen had nothing to criticize and everything to be worried about. Her only daughter was quite clearly marrying a man who knew himself and his values well enough to be certain of his standards. John Graves could not and would not be easily moved away from those standards toward others, no matter how important those others might seem to his new mother-in-law.

I was, I must say, delighted. I still am. I think of those cocktail parties almost every time John and I meet.

Which we have done infrequently. Jean and I have visited the "ranch" in Glen Rose twice, and Jane has come east frequently. But John has not. His visit to Key West was the first time since he married Jane that I saw him outside of Texas. And it was the tarpon, not I, that brought him.

In the early morning of the second day of our three-day charter with Jeffrey, a tarpon took John Graves's brown Cockroach fly and slammed across the flats ripping more than two hundred feet of backing off the reel on the Number 9 Sage fly rod John had made for himself in the shed alongside his barn in Glen Rose. Two hours later in the high May sun that had, by then, heated the humid air to close to ninety degrees, the fish was still on and it was in better shape than John. At least, watching the sweat roll from his brow, I thought so. The tarpon could still jump; John could hardly move. Looking at his steely gray hair along the nape of his seasoned neck, watching the hard-knuckled and calloused hands kink and curl from the cramps that came from holding the rod for 120 minutes or more, seeing him blink his one good eye to clear the sweat from his vision, I realized that this was a fight the fish might win.

But John Graves hadn't changed in thirty-five years. Just as stubborn, just as ornery, and just as proud as he had always been, he hung in there. Three hours and ten minutes after the tarpon first ate the fly, Jeffrey released him. Although the ninety-pound fish was weary, it did not need as much caring as many tarpon Jeffrey has revived and released.

"That's a lovely rod, John," said Jeffrey, after the tarpon had vanished in the channel, "but I think it's a little light for this kind of fishing."

"Jeffrey," sighed John as he slumped to a seat, "you're right."

Cruising slowly through the channel from north to south, Jeffrey shut down the Yamaha when we reached the Marquesas' south shore and anchored in eight feet of water above a large patch of pale marl. The bowl-shaped depression gleamed under the one o'clock sun, a ladle of transparent tropical sea unmarred by vegetation, a coral dish as delicately vacant as a porcelain soup tureen polished and waiting on a mahogany sideboard. Jeffrey lowered his small mushroom anchor carefully and the *Waterlight* swung in the current on a surface as still as cut glass. In the windless torpor, each of our spirits slumped along with John. Released from the stretch of the tensions that had tugged for three hours, we were quite ready to do nothing but sit there, accepting the sun's potent presence while we regrouped for the afternoon.

"We'll have some lunch," Jeffrey said, opening his ice chest. "If a tarpon or two does cruise across this white spot, we'll see it coming. One of you should be ready to cast."

No one moved, so I took my rod from its brackets and laid it along the broad gunwale, Cockroach fly at the ready.

"Be sure you drink plenty of fluids," Jeffrey advised as he passed around ice water, beers, and jugs of Gatorade, "especially you, John Graves. In this sun, you can get dehydrated more quickly than you think."

Sitting on the casting deck, my legs draped over the bow so my toes just touched the water's surface, I joined the general silence as each of us foraged on our tunafish-salad sandwiches. In the flooding tide, the *Waterlight* swung on her mooring so her bow faced seaward; my view as I gulped my Gatorade reached to the southern horizon across an ocean as peaceful and green as a croquet lawn. Not a riffle stirred in the unusual afternoon calm, no short seas had been left by any long-gone gale, not even a vestige of a swell nudged the tranquil surface to announce its parent storm a thousand miles at sea.

Over my years of fishing, especially on those trips aboard the *Double Trouble* with Matty, I have become conditioned to scanning every sea for signals. Some flags raised from below are as dramatic and unmistakable as the black, new-moon crescent of a swordfish dorsal. Others appear more frequently: white puffs of feeding bluefish as they break water; raindrop patterns of tiny baitfish pursuing an invisible purpose; or the spreading V of a fish wake as some unidentifiable shape swims just beneath the surface. Since my first days on the water, I have been a lucky fish spotter; I have become accustomed to having others doubt my reports simply because they have not seen what my eyes recorded. Knowing this, I was careful not to overstate my case on that somnolent afternoon at anchor. But about a half-mile offshore, something unusual was happening. Of that, I was convinced.

Along the horizon a spreading banner of darker blue flowed like indigo spilled across a lime-green canvas. Some massive, submerged turbulence roiled the flawless surface, altered its refraction, and changed its hue.

"See that, Jeffrey," I called. "Is that a bunch of fish out there, or is it a breeze about to take hold?"

"I don't know," he answered, making it clear by his tone even he could not solve a mystery so distant, so ill defined.

I kept my eyes on the spreading strangeness. When a tarpon leapt free of the sea, a silver missile fired from a submerged ship, and hung there against the sky at least six feet above the horizon line, I gasped and shouted, my voice charged and the words tumbling even as the fish turned on its side in the air and crashed in a welter of white water.

"It's a tarpon, a big tarpon. Did you see it, Jeffrey, did you?"

By the time my question took shape and Jeffrey was framing his response, the query was rendered academic. From the dark pasture at least six tarpon leaped, and then six more and then others until an incredible tapestry was woven for us by countless giant silver fish. Like a surging school of bluefish or herring grown to monstrous dimensions, tarpon churned, jumped, rolled, pushed water, and leapt again and again, wanting, it seemed, to take wing, to depart the very sea they swam in.

"Sharks! Hammerheads!" Jeffrey yelled. "It's sharks

chasing a big school of tarpon. They're driving them like sheep."

In our silence, watching, knowing even then that we were witness to a natural cataclysm few humans will ever see, we could hear a sound—a ripping, as if a vast cotton sheet was being torn from edge to edge. It was the sound of the sea's rending, the hiss of panic as hundreds of tarpon swam at their ultimate and desperate speed. As we watched and listened, the sound acquired new tones, more depth, until it became close to a roar, more like a waterfall's cascade than fabric pulled asunder.

Thrashing, pounding their tails convulsively in the hysteria of their flight, the school of thousands of great tarpon flailed the still surface so violently that the liquid rumble filled the air around us with an awesome echo of distant, rolling thunder. Driven closer to us by still unseen sharks, the silver and indigo mass began changing color under its dapple of white water that marked each breaking fish. A copper-burnt-orange rose began blooming at the center of the violence, spreading its somber petals until they, too, were a piece of the whole.

"That's blood," Jeffrey said. "Those fish are being torn to pieces."

A new sound made its entrance, one I knew immediately, one every boatman knows: the sibilance of a breaking sea, a wave on the approach. But here? Here in a dead calm.

The wave rolled toward us with surprising speed. Perfectly formed, gleaming in the shimmering sunlight, it crested at almost two feet, lifted the *Waterlight* as it surged under and past us and crumpled into white water as it stumbled against the shallows of the flats. It was a wave born of apocalypse, a creation of fear, a signal of massacre and futile

189

flight, an echo of the final energies expended by slaughtered tarpon and their relentless butchers.

Herding their silver sheep, the sharks pressed toward the Marquesas shoals, knowing their work would be quicker once the tarpon were forced against the flats.

A dark dorsal, curved and blunt, cut the water as I watched and understood I was seeing a shark, not a tarpon. I was stunned by its speed. Peering from pulpits off Montauk, I have watched many sharks move out of harm's way. There was always a certain languor to their departure, as if they understood the immensity of the depths at their disposal. And I have watched sharks cruising the flats and witnessed their strikes at hooked and wounded fish. But even then, these predators moved with deliberate speed, certain of their ultimate success.

This hammerhead was a projectile. A roostertail of white water flared from its dorsal as emphatically as it would from a high-speed outboard. The massive shadow shape beneath raced across the bleached flats like a shaft of dark light. I could not absorb the concept; the notion that a submerged creature that large could move so quickly stunned me. There could, I knew, be no defense, no evasion of such startling speed. A new standard of wild behavior had been set. I watched and knew I would judge the flight of every other fish by the mark that shark etched in my memory.

Once pushed against the land, the tarpon scattered, followed by their pursuers. There was no longer a concentration of doom. Only the faltering copper rose still bloomed offshore to affirm the spectacle each of us knew had been ours alone, and would always be. We could, we knew, return to this place, to these Marquesas each May day for the rest of our lives and never witness such a spectacle again.

Nevertheless, I sought verification. "Have you ever seen anything like that?" I asked Jeffrey.

"No," he said, shaking his head, "no, never."

Sitting quietly, more weary now than we were before we anchored for lunch, we waited for our adrenalin rush to subside. It seemed almost surreal to be so taut in what is thought to be a torpid climate.

Within a half-hour, however, we had revived and chattered easily about the spectacle, John's long battle, and the tarpon's migratory mysteries.

Jane, I noticed, seemed restless.

"Can I slip overboard for a swim?" she asked Jeffrey, and then explained. "All those fluids you made sure we drank are beginning to get to me. I'll just hang on to the boat and do what I have to do, okay?"

"Sure, fine. Do what you need to, Jane. We'll make sure you get back aboard."

Jane stood, her mouth set firmly in that line of determination I know so well, sweat beading on her forehead above her large, brown eyes. I watched to see just how she would, in her late middle age, trim though she might be, negotiate her entrance to the waters of this Marquesas lagoon.

"John," she said to me, in a tone I also know well, "you don't have to watch my every move. Isn't there something else you can do?"

As I turned toward the bow, Jeffrey said, "You might want to wait a minute or two, Jane, before you go over. Look there, about six o'clock, coming toward the stern."

Following the line set by Jeffrey's extended arm we each looked toward the eastern edge of our coral-dish anchorage. There, outlined in dark and dramatic silhouette against the white sand was the distinctive profile of a large hammerhead moving directly toward the *Waterlight*. This fish was in no hurry. Quite the opposite. Apparently assured of its complete command of any situation, the shark took possession of the small lagoon. With sinuous, lazy motions as fluid as the currents it moved through, the hammerhead continued its sensual and silent advance until it was directly under our boat.

"God, isn't it beautiful," Jeffrey said in a half-whisper.

I judged the shark to be a foot longer than our flats skiff, which made it at least an eighteen-foot hammerhead, by far the most magnificent and terrifying I have ever seen. Its nearness was even more exceptional. In the sun's glare, I could see each of its luminous, green eyes at each end of the odd airfoil protuberances that extended from its snout. An oddity familiar to saltwater fishermen, the hammerhead's profile had sometimes seemed clumsy to me, a kind of genetic flaw, a handicap. But looking down at that fish less than four feet from us in water as clear as if it were distilled, the hammerhead's most distinctive feature seemed more awesome than awkward, fitting, not freakish.

Hesitating a moment in the darkness of the *Waterlight*'s shadow, the shark appeared to be deliberating its immediate choices. None of us made a sound. Then, with a subtle movement of its sweeping tail, the hammerhead glided across the lagoon onto the flats where we could see its dorsal above water and then back into the channel further west where it vanished in the darker, deeper unknowns.

Jane spoke first. "Jeffrey," she asked, "have you got a can, or a bucket or something I can use?"

During the next two days that John and Jane visited with us, staying in the small apartment built above a storage shed in the backyard of our rented home on South Street, I talked with John several times about our days on the water, sharks, and fly fishing. I learned that he was almost totally committed to the fly rod, using it even when angling for the small bass and perch in the creek running through his ranch and in his dug stock pond called in Texas style a "tank."

Typically, he had thought a great deal about that commitment. And, typically, he had assembled a scholar's library of information on every aspect of the skill. He had learned to make his own rods, tie his own flies, and research his own ichthyological data, and had even begun thinking about how he would convert a plain, empty boat hull into a flats skiff. He is a fellow who goes all the way with his avocations.

I was ready to listen to his ideas. "It's an infirmity without a cure, fly fishing," he said at one point. "But it's also a pretty deep field of study, bottomless really, which I guess is why it attracts a lot of bookish types, including ex-professors like me. The first symptom is a desire to cast a fly nicely like somebody you've seen somewhere, maybe on a trout river in the Rockies. To lay the line out straight to a reasonable distance, and have the fly land where you want it to. And that may be the easiest part of the whole damned business."

"Ah, yes," I said with some bitterness. "Very easy indeed."

"Then you start throwing flies at fish," said John, "which arouses your curiosity about the kinds of water different species prefer, and what they like to eat. Which in turn, unless you're careful, leads you into trying to imitate what they eat with hair and fur and feathers and tinsel and thread."

"Fly tying," I said.

"By then there is no escape, and all the rest of it follows. Building rods that will help you cast better, you hope. Messing with boats. Learning about knots and splices and tapered lines and leaders, not to mention all the kinds of fish there are to read about and try to catch, one species after another. All of it follows the simple, fatal fact that you once admired the motions of some lunatic sloshing around in cold river water and waving a thin pole in the air."

"You're sorry you got involved, then?"

"Hell, no, I'm not," John said. "What I'm sorry about is that it took me this long to get around to trying it in salt water. Except that it's great to be hitting a whole new realm of the sport. You know something? At our age, there is no earthly way you and I are going to live long enough to learn all there is to know about this kind of fly fishing. Isn't that a pretty thought?"

"I may have had some prettier ones from time to time," I answered. "What about other kinds of fishing?"

"Fishing's fishing," said my brother-in-law. "I don't mind throwing a baited hook at catfish when I want one to eat. Sometimes I'll switch to spinning gear if the wind gets to blowing a gale. But it's not the same; it's not as good."

"After watching you and Jeffrey fly fish, I'm inclined to agree with that," I said. "But I still don't know *why* the other ways aren't as good."

"Well, they're fine unless you're a diseased fly man, I guess. I don't know why I believe fly fishing is better, not really. It's got something to do with *grace,* I think—with handling rather simple tools that feel good and get to working like a part of you, so that using fly tackle is an active and satisfying thing even when you don't catch anything. It's cleaner, too, somehow, and single fly hooks with the barbs mashed down are a hell of a lot easier than trebles on fish that break off, or the ones you bring in and release. I don't often keep them any more, do you?"

"No, not often," I said, thinking that my answer didn't matter much at that point. It had been a while since I'd brought a fish near enough to have to make a decision. "I believe most of what you say, John, except that I don't find fly casting to be nearly as easy as you seem to think it is. And I've got a bunch of good spinning rods and reels."

"Keep on using them," John said, and then grinned. "But if you'll learn how to throw a fly right, I bet you'll be giving that spinning gear to Roger. Get some books and videos and practice casting on the grass or somewhere. Did you ever see that casting tape of Lefty Krch's?"

"Yeah, I've seen it," I said, telling him the same lie I'd told elsewhere. Watching me fly cast on the Upsalquitch, in Alaska, on the Leirasveit or the Kennebec, a half-dozen other fly fishermen had asked the same question. Evidently, all I had to do was pick up a rod to indicate I was seriously lacking in instruction. Shit, I told myself now, I don't need to watch a television tape to learn how to cast a fly. But I knew it could help, and that made me even more angry with myself.

"Well, it's a good piece of teaching," he said. "I wouldn't nudge at you about this except that I know you've got the bug. Practice, damn it; decent casting doesn't amount to much. Practice every day. It'll just come to you at some point and you'll wonder why it ever seemed hard. Grace, Brother John, grace will come to you from on high. Amen."

"Amen, Brother John," I said.

Jane and John left early the next morning. That afternoon, I took my big tarpon fly rod down to the White Street pier and practiced. Hey, give it a shot, I told myself. Who knows, you might even catch a tarpon.

A month later, I was still trying and had just one chance left. Knowing Jean and I were due to leave for Maine late that June, I arranged a final trip to the Marquesas with

Jeffrey. Roger came with us on a majestic morning just three days before the summer solstice—long days that arrived in the small hours and lasted until even the most continental visitors had finished their alfresco dinners on the Bagatelle's verandah.

We were up at four, bumping each other in the cramped kitchen, making certain we had packed proper lunches. Since he left high school, Roger has not spent many nights sleeping. Which does not mean he is alert at dawn. On the contrary, his nocturnal ramblings along Key West's restless streets and his silent and determined alcohol intake set him up for sunup surliness. But fishing dulls his churl, and knowing he could rest for an hour once we set our course from Garrison Bight gave him hope.

Like a marionette whose strings go slack, he rolled with the *Waterlight*'s turns, eyes closed, blond-haired head nodding like a sunflower in a breeze. His gentle face with its button nose and boy's mouth looked, as always, angelic in repose—an altar boy at rest. Which is, I suppose, why an altar boy's disguise has so often been used by scoundrels.

I wanted to nudge the slim figure, give him no peace, make him able to receive the glorious messages that dawn was sending us. Even as Jeffrey peered west through the dark, sweeping the sea for the few modest markers that line the all but invisible trail through the lakes, I could look off our stern and watch the dawn's pale tints dilute the darkness on the eastern horizon. Soon enough light had spilled to silhouette morning wings as herons, gulls, and comorants began their early errands. Alone in my world of sound, speed, and genuine solitude I wanted, as I always do on that journey through the water wilderness, to take someone's hand, to share the glories we alone were being given.

But Roger was not about to be that person. His concentration on recuperation was absolute and he did not stir

196

until Jeffrey throttled down and began to use his quiet electric motors to move us along the Marquesas' southern shore where tarpon sometimes gather early on a new day. I made Roger fish first. My perversity sprang partially from my knowledge of the weight of his beer-battered head and my feeling that there were indeed tarpon to be had. I wanted to see Roger react to a strike that stripped two hundred feet of backing off his spinning reel.

In twenty minutes, Jeffrey had put us alongside a school. The fish were daisy-chaining in a casual circle, quite unaware of their visitors. Roger, however, was overly aware of the lumbering, coppery shoulders that emerged from an ocean that had yet to become blue with daylight. In the windless dawn, the sibilant hiss of the fish sounded soft on the morning as the tarpon exhaled air from their flotation bladders. Even their sliding silver emergence and entry to and from the sea could be heard, that most fragile sound of those ultra-smooth, silver-scaled torsos sliding along the warm salt surface.

"Cast now!" Jeffrey said, his crisp voice cutting the paralysis Roger and I shared as we watched the splendid pageant just off our bow.

Raising his rod, Roger's arm pivoted in the school's general direction, but no plug hit the water.

"Shit," Roger said, flipping the bail that he had forgotten and casting again.

"Reel slowly," Jeffrey called from the stern.

Roger stopped reeling and the red-and-white plug wobbled to the surface, followed by a wide-open tarpon mouth as large and as dark as a black bushel basket. "Oh, God," Roger said, then yanked hard. Soaring free of the surface, the plug whipped empty air above Roger's head, snapped back, wrapping line around the rod tip on its rebound. Reaching for the tip, Roger tried to untangle the mess of monofilament, then put the rod on the deck when he realized the complexity of his problem. As he worked, frowning and fumbling, tarpon circled like porpoises for a few more moments and then vanished as gentle ripples radiated from the scene of their dawn frolic.

Gentle Jeffrey said nothing. Unlike so many professional fishing guides, who, I suppose, sometimes feel demeaned by their for-hire status, he never tries even to the score by criticizing an inept fisherman. He does just the opposite: he tries harder to make sure that fisherman is successful.

Poling the *Waterlight* along the south shore, past the entrance to the deepest channel, Jeffrey let his skiff drift into the same coral serving dish we had anchored in four weeks before. I had not forgotten the hammerhead, nor the venue of its visit.

"We'll try it here a few minutes, Roger," Jeffrey said. "Be ready to cast when I tell you. These fish will be traveling, not daisy-chaining."

Sighing with remorse at his earlier showing, Roger stood at attention on the bow casting platform. Believing that I had given him a fair opportunity to hook up, I picked up my fly rod and stood at the stern quarter, just in case. Jeffrey stayed in the bow, ready to instruct if and when he saw a fish turn Roger's way.

Incredibly, as I stared off to the northern sky, my eyes caught the movement of three shapes heading toward us off the flats, not from the deeper water as Jeffrey anticipated.

They came closer, moving steadily, but not quickly. The composure of their procession told me that they had not seen our boat, or, if they had, they judged it no threat.

On they came. I began shaking. My knees, as they always do when I see large fish, deserted their structural purpose. I had trouble staying upright. Even if I had wanted to, which I did not, I could hardly have gotten a word past my tight windpipe.

The tarpon, because that is what they definitely were, never swerved or hesitated. They were, I could tell, going to glide just a few feet from where I stood.

I began swinging my rod in its casting arc, stripping line as I did. Any idiot could cast far enough to reach these fish, I told myself. For Christ's sake, they were practically under our stern.

There were three of them. The two in front were smaller. The single fish, a few lengths back, looked immense. I cast in their general direction.

My fly flopped on the water. By the time it sank to the tarpons' depth, the two lead fish had already moved too far toward the bow. But that third fish found a Cockroach sinking slowly just in front of its mouth. Opening its maw, the tarpon inhaled my fly. I saw it vanish.

When I did, I yanked hard. The fish kept swimming, and that's what saved me. It was the tarpon's progress, not my strike, that did the deed. Before the fish recognized the fly for what it was, its own forward motion snapped the hook against the corner of its jaws.

"Hey!" I yelled, "Hey!"

Spinning, Jeffrey turned toward the stern, saw what was happening, saw the fish dash under the bow and saw the bend in my rod.

Then each of us watched open-mouthed as the tarpon jumped clear less than twenty feet off the bow, crashing back in an awkward, sideways tumble that sounded like a cellar door thrown overboard.

Then that fish took off.

"It's a big fish, a big fish, John!" Jeffrey yelled from the brink of his composure.

"Get up here in the bow," he called as he cleared a

path. Holding my rod so its tip pointed at the sky, I edged forward, stepped up onto the platform. The fish made it easier than it might have been. Its run appeared endless, unswerving, and fast. Line disappeared from the Fin-Nor fly-casting reel a generous soul had given me, and I began to be certain the backing would vanish entirely. Nothing I could do could stop the fish, not with a twelve-pound-test tippet tied between the shock leader and my flyline. There was no surge, no struggle. Line left me as if the other end was fast to a heavily loaded trailer truck cruising a throughway downgrade at seventy miles an hour.

Just when I was certain that tarpon's first run was also my last, the fish jumped. I could not comprehend the distance. At first, I thought it was some other fish, not mine. Far to the west, on the way to the Tortugas, the tarpon leapt free and clear, hung there and crashed back.

The line went slack.

"He's off," I said.

"No. No," Jeffrey said. "He's headed straight back this way. Reel, John. Reel as fast as you can."

I tried. I turned the crank as fast as my hand and wrist would respond to my brain's message. I could not catch up to the fish. Slack line curved on the water's surface.

"Reel! Reel!" Jeffrey yelled.

I did, desperately. Then, pressure, wonderful pressure. The encounter continued. I could feel the fish; it could feel me. Once again, we were joined. What I'd said to my father was right: fishing should come first.

"Flyline coming in," Jeffrey called.

I had retrieved all the backing. My aching arm told me it had been a job.

Just as the flyline began to build on the reel, the tarpon turned and began another run: the same truck on the same throughway.

This time, it hit a wall. The reel stopped turning, the rod bent sharply, too sharply. I watched, knowing disaster had been born in that instant of silence. The rod snapped back in my hand like a tree branch bent and released. This time each of us knew the fish was free.

"What happened?" Jeffrey asked.

Looking at the reel I knew. When the fish had turned and run toward me, and when I was reeling in as fast as I possibly could, the slack in the line had looped back on itself. I had, in fact, wrapped a free-floating loop of backing around the reel. On its next run, the tarpon had gone as far as that loop. Wrapped around the line, it became an instant brake, a stop as effective as any knot. The tippet, as it was designed to do, broke under the pressure. My tarpon was free. My giant tarpon, gone.

"A big fish," Jeffrey said. "A very big fish."

"Hey," I said, "it took my fly. I cast to it by myself and it took my fly. That's the first tarpon that's ever done that."

Nine months ago, that happened, and I can still see that fish leaping against the sky, almost as far off as the Tortugas.

We are fishing inside the lagoon today, in barracuda country. When February's northeast winds chill the deeper waters of the channels, barracuda congregate in the thin water of the Marquesas flats favoring circles of pale sand free of turtle grass and seaweed. From his perch on the poling platform above the stern, Jeffrey looks for their motionless cigar shapes; these fish take the sun as studiously as a Manhattan broker on his first day alongside a Miami Beach hotel pool.

"Fish at twelve o'clock," Jeffrey calls. "He's out of casting range, but let me know when you can see him."

Staring, peering straight ahead, I see the barracuda's

shadow profile suspended above the golden sand. "I see him. I see him." I raise my rod and begin false casting, the lime-green tassel whipping back and forth.

"Cast now," Jeffrey tells me, and I do.

The line collapses on the surface as if it spilled from an overhead slop jar. The fly is nowhere near the fish.

"Pick it up and cast again," Jeffrey says. "He's still right there."

I yank too hard on my retrieve. The fly pops from the surface headed straight for me. I duck as it wraps itself around the rod. By now, the *Waterlight*'s easy momentum has brought the boat too close and the barracuda glides off.

Jeffrey says nothing, keeps poling, keeps looking.

Half-an-hour later, after a discouraging series of flawed and fruitless casts, I think I detect a note of weary resignation in Jeffrey's words, encouraging though they may be. He has, after all, put me within casting range of a half-dozen sturdy barracuda, all of whom are still at large and at ease.

"Fish at ten o'clock," he calls, "moving toward eleven."

I see the fish, and I cast. The fly lands almost where I want it to go, but I begin stripping line, trying to retrieve it as fast as possible so I can try the cast a second time.

"He sees the fly," Jeffrey calls. "He's after it. Here he comes. Keep stripping. Strip as fast as you can."

Now I can see the push of water racing behind my fly as the barracuda gets up to speed. Then I see the fish. It is less than twenty feet from our bow and racing.

I keep stripping. I watch as the barracuda opens its mouth and eats my fly. I expect the fish to strike the boat. It turns and runs a few feet, then jumps. The sun flashes on its sides of mottled silver.

202

"Look at that jump," yells Jeffrey. "Get him on the reel, John. Get him on the reel."

As the fish runs across the flats, I keep tension on the flyline with my left hand. In moments, the slack is taken.

"You got him on the reel. Good boy," Jeffrey yells.

The fish makes several jumps, at least three fine runs, and then I have it beside the boat: my first barracuda on a fly. Jeffrey leans over the gunwale and cautiously removes the hook. After a motionless moment, the barracuda waves its tail gently and moves off at a measured pace across the flats.

Jeffrey walks forward and shakes my hand. "Congratulations, Cap," he says. "That was a good fish, about fifteen pounds."

Jean is smiling as I put down my rod and slide onto the seat beside her.

"How about some lunch?" asks Jeffrey. Not waiting for our answer, he opens a cooler and passes around sandwiches and cold juice. Staked off, the *Waterlight* is the only boat inside the Marquesas lagoon, we are the only human souls in sight. Because I know this is a wilderness preserve and because Key West is more than twenty miles northeast, I feel privileged, lucky to be in this wild and distant place on such a sparkling adventure on such a fine, sun-drenched day.

"There," I say to Jean, as I remember John Graves's words, "I've caught a barracuda on a fly. Next will come a tarpon, then a bonefish, and then a permit. Isn't that a wonderful agenda to have in front of me. It took me sixty-five years to get this far. I'm going to have a shitload of fun traveling the rest of the way."

And we hold hands.

Key West

December 7, 1988

In the late afternoon when I first heard the news forty-seven years ago, I was in Pippy Landon's Madison Avenue apartment. "Alone with a mature woman," was how I often described such situations to my classmates when I explained how I spent my weekends in Manhattan. Describing Pippy as mature was my first exaggeration; she was, I think, about a year older than I. Intimating intimacy was a much more blatant prevarication; Pippy was a "nice girl," to use my mother's phrase, and in 1941 "nice girls didn't do that," to borrow Joe Sewall's line about the virtuous teasers of his and my college years.

She and I were drinking Dubonnet on the rocks, nibbling unadorned crackers, and listening to radio music when we heard the announcement that everyone who was alive that day will never forget: "Planes of the Japanese air force have bombed the U.S. Navy base at Pearl Harbor . . ." I finished my drink, said goodbye, and walked to Grand Central to catch the next train to New Haven. I haven't seen Pippy Landon since.

But I have thought of her at least once a year for forty-seven years. And today, in my mind's eye, I can still see her wide grey eyes growing even wider as she realized the impact of that news bulletin. How incongruous it is, here in Key West Harbor aboard the *Waterlight,* to transport myself through time to that lowering, cold evening in the city. And how lucky I am to be where I am, to have survived so much, to have this morning open like a rose. At sunup, this island's overstuffed cumulus marched across the new sky, towering, ripe, and carrying round grey sacks full of showers on their bulging shoulders. For an hour or two, I thought we would have to cancel the short trip I'd planned with Jeffrey. But as we gathered at the small dock at Garrison Bight, patches of blue opened in the east above the schlock of Roosevelt Drive.

"Sam," I said, putting my arm across his strong, broad back, "it's going to be an okay day." He nodded, pleased that I was pleased and relatively unconcerned about the weather. Sam abides. The youngest of four gentle sons, he is the most gentle, always has been. Even after twenty-five years of growing up in a nation rattled by tremor after tremor, he maintains a stolid optimism, a kind of unswerving confidence that the day he is about to start will bring him good fortune. Quite a few have not, but they have had no effect on Sam's blue-eyed affection for life, his unshakable faith in the essential goodness of man and nature—nature most of all.

He arrived in Key West four days ago with Ellen, his lady, from Portland. Together, they have done the town, been to the Raw Bar for conch chowder, gone fishing aboard the *Waterlight.* That was on their second day, a day full of wind and whitecaps that pushed Jeffrey away from any serious plans. We fished in the lee, casting feather jigs in the channels for enough gray snappers to have for dinner, a dinner Jeffrey cooked, dropping whole, scaled and spiced fish into a super-hot frying pan sizzling with his boiling-oil

206

recipe. With cold wine, outdoors under the stars and bougainvillea, those snapper were ambrosia touched with the romance of knowing we had brought our meal home from the sea a few hours before.

Sam and Ellen leave tomorrow and I wanted one day, or at least part of a day, on the flats. I wanted Sam, as I want each person I love, to know the vitality, the excitement, and the rare beauty of the flats in this particular sea where the Gulf and the Atlantic meet. As he often does, Jeffrey recognized my hopes and made space in his schedule.

There was not time for a full day, so we are working the flats close to home: two particular ones close enough to the city to surprise many fishermen, even some who claim to know these waters. Jeffrey has staked us off a short cast from the edge of a flat and Sam is on the bow, blind casting a green tube lure. A fine athlete and an experienced spin caster, he can cast almost as far as Jeffrey. As always, Sam is trusting. He can see no fish, has never seen a barracuda, and does not know what to expect. But he has his instructions and he follows them with patience and diligence, making certain the water is covered and trying his competitive best to retrieve the lure as quickly as Jeffrey insists he should. I am praying for a strike, or at least a follower, any fish who will send a signal that this is not a fool's game Sam is playing.

Jeffrey sees the fish first. "Reel, Sam!" he says. "Keep reeling as fast as you can. He's after it."

Sam. What a fine student. He reels, and reels as fast as he possibly can, and keeps reeling until the tube lure is less than two feet from the boat. Then Sam swings his rod across the bow to keep the lure moving. At the last possible second, when it is so close to the boat I think its teeth will hit our bow and not the tube, the barracuda strikes.

White water erupts. Sam's rod bows. Line whistles through the guides as the fish steams off across the flats.

Then the barracuda jumps. Four feet clear of the pale water its three-foot silver log of a torso gleams in the sunlight, pauses there, then falls, vanishes.

"Hey!" Sam yells. "Wow!" And yells again. "What a fish!"

I'll say. I am absolutely gratified at this good fortune. Strong as he is, Sam knows and acknowledges the strength, mystery, and wonder at the other of the thread that connects him to this universe.

In ten minutes, the barracuda is alongside, in Jeffrey's hands. Hooks are gently removed, the fish held clear of the water for a final instant, a last look from Sam and a photograph to certify this, his first fish from the flats.

Sam is, I think to myself, forty years ahead of me, which is fine. I haven't wasted those years; I came to the flats later in life than he. This is, after all, what fathers ought to be about: saving years of their children's lives.

"Let's travel the back country," I suggest after Ellen has taken her turn casting. "These two ought to see how much there is to see just a few minutes from Key West."

Jeffrey heads northeast, threading the thin-water channels that lace the thousands of mangrove hummocks and small keys scattered on the shoal that spills 125 miles of greens, blues, whites, and yellows from Key West to Homestead. We see no other boats as we wind through the wilderness maze. At thirty knots or better in a small boat that planes as effortlessly as the *Waterlight,* the sensation of speed is heightened by the nearness of the apple-green walls of sea grape and mangrove that blanket both sides of a narrow aquamarine channel between two hummocks. Banking sharply around a channel bend, the boat scatters flights of great white herons, egrets, cormorants, ibis, kingfisher, osprey, skimmers, gulls, and man o'war birds. Like petals on the wind, they swirl above us, so close that we could touch them if we tried.

It is difficult for me to believe there is another water-scape like this one. Where else, I wonder, could there be the combination of warm salt-sea tides, cobalt depths, lime-green shallows, jade foliage, and the pure loneliness that shelters so many hundreds of sprawling square miles. How much this waterscape has to give; how much it has given me.

Scenes from past trips flicker as the roar of Jeffrey's engine isolates each of us in our deafness. I see a great tarpon leap from its Marquesas channel, my fly in the corner of its boiler-plate jaw. And then the moment when I knew all was lost, the instant the flyline tangled around the rod butt, slipped to the junction where reel and rod meet where it was cut by the reel's own rim: fish lost, flyline lost, all lost. My second tarpon on a fly, my second tarpon catastrophe, witnessed for the second time by Jeffrey. On this December 7 anniversary of a nation's catastrophe, I count the months, weeks, and days until I will have a chance to redeem myself, redeem all.

As if I needed a remonstrance from the gods, the heavens opened on our way home from that May 25th calamity. With thunderous majesty, cumulus darker than night strode from the north on waters scuffed by an advance guard of rain squalls and slapping winds. When the awesome center of the storm struck, it caught the *Waterlight* on her passage across the al-ready tormented surface of the Boca Grande Channel.

Slammed at us by wind gusts clocked at sixty-five mph, a horizontal deluge plunged from black skies. Mixed with gale-driven salt spray, the torrent literally blinded me, pelted my eyes with such brutal force that I could not see the boat's bow. With my head bowed under rolling thunder and slashing lightning, I could not conceive how Jeffrey could peer into the tempest and find enough space to steer by.

But he stayed on course, took us inside islands and hummocks, finding some shelter in their lee. I could see only the deck between my feet, a deck constantly awash with seas that punched and cuffed us, a heavyweight storm that had our lightweight boat on the ropes, battering us at will.

The one-hour trip home took more than two and when we reached Garrison Bight each of us was drenched. My eyes stung so from their immersion, their beating, that I could hardly see, although the rain had tapered off and the restless winds had become less violent. Even after a hot shower at home, the storm stayed with me; it was another day before my eyes stopped smarting. But even the dramatic vision of that darkness at noon could not obscure the remembered lurch of disappointment that tumbled me when that flyline snapped and my tarpon abandoned me without so much as a farewell wave.

How different that day was from this. Still blessed by an overhead sun, the *Waterlight* slows, glides to a silent drift across a broad stretch of white sand covered by water less than two feet deep. After the roar of the trip through the hummocks, the silence and the space are stunning.

"We may see a lemon shark on these flats," Jeffrey says. "Sometimes they will take a lure. Be ready to cast, Ellen."

A half-hour slips by. Except for one small barracuda, the flats seem barren.

"I'm not doing too well as a guide, am I," Jeffrey says. "I was here the other day and saw several lemons."

We have drifted a mile now, and still the pale flats unfold, an alabaster scroll that keeps its secrets. Then each of us sees the black velvet shape, sinuous against the luminous

210

background. "There's a shark," Jeffrey says, "a lemon shark, about five feet." Pausing, he shouts this time: "Look over there. Eleven o'clock. It's a school of sharks. There must be twenty of them."

We float toward them, and they glide toward us, scores of curling, dark shadows against the pearly marl, a procession charged with mystery, a silent gathering of grace, a presence of sea creatures so completely wild, so unexplained and unexpected, and yet so dramatically visible that none of us can ever forget this moment of discovery.

I am so grateful for their procession. I want so much for Sam and Ellen, for everyone, to witness just such a statement of the wonder that is this place. If enough of us can record these moments, then each of us will fight to save such places. And especially the generation that is Sam's and Ellen's, the generation that now stands between these places and the forces that threaten them. Each of us who shares these glories owes that defense, myself most of all. Because I recognize how much these flats have given me, and how much they still have to give to tens of thousands of others, I am committed to do whatever I can to make men see these places for the rare and wonderful mystery they are.

Today, the lemon sharks have helped. Our casts in their direction spook the school. In moments, they are gone.

Jeffrey poles to a channel, starts the outboard and heads for home along what was once the final stretch of the old inland waterway. As we approach Garrison Bight Channel, the clouds that had welcomed the sunrise roll in again, darkening the afternoon. The sun, it seems, shone just long enough to brighten our adventure.

I've had more than my share of that sort of luck.

211

Key West

January 22, 1989

A little over a decade ago, for reasons that have always eluded me, I was invited to speak to the annual Thanksgiving Dinner meeting of the New England Society of New York. I suppose my position as a past New Yorker and present Maine journalist qualified me; little else did. Nevertheless, there were several reasons I was pleased to be invited. The dinner was a black-tie production held in the ballroom of the Plaza Hotel—a place that my brother Chick and I know better than most. During the years when we were on the list of young gentlemen who qualified for invitations to the debutante balls held during the holiday season, we spent most of our nights in the Plaza ballroom. When we weren't invited, we went anyway; we knew how to slip through an unmarked door off the Palm Court, climb some back stairs, and emerge in a hallway at the back of that splendid second-story ballroom.

After more than thirty-five years off the circuit, I wanted to make a nostalgic visit, and the New England Society banquet seemed an appropriate occasion. Dressed in a dinner jacket, I would be in my proper drinking uniform

213

and I'd been told Society functions were spiffy affairs with plenty of good wine and fine food.

During our stay in the city, Jean and I were guests of my Uncle Henry's. He and Aunt Katherine had a comfortable Fifth Avenue apartment overlooking the park, and the setting was right in tune with the purpose of our visit. Besides, I wanted to see Uncle Henry. My father's younger brother, he had followed his older sibling to Manhattan from Durham, North Carolina, where my grandfather was a Methodist minister. "Come on up, Henry," my father had written, "there are a bunch of rich Yankee women here and they just love southern boys."

Within two years of his arrival, Henry had married Aunt Katherine, who fit my father's description, and then some. For the rest of his long and happy life, the Unc played his role as a southern boy. Fifty years in the big city left not a mark on his Carolina inflections, and five decades of life in high society never laid a hand on Henry's personna as a fun-loving mischief-maker from Dixie who dared dour Yankees to disapprove.

So there was nothing for it but to bring him along to the Plaza. No sooner had he heard the name, New England Society of New York, but he announced his membership in its sister organization, the North Carolina Society of New York and allowed as how that entitled him to a place at the table.

Off we went, the four of us, properly duded and on time. Almost eighty, the Unc had lost just a bit of his speed. But I knew he had lost none of his love of mischief, and I was half-concerned about what he might do and half-excited by the prospect that he might do something.

When some 250 properly tight-lipped Yankees had finished their pre-dinner drinks and seated themselves at the Plaza's finest dinner tables spread with glittering china and

214

crystal, the Society's chairman stood and announced that Father So-and-So would bless us all. The minister, as it happened, sat at Henry's table. The clergyman rose and rolled along a sonorous trail of benedictions before he arrived at the spot where he announced that the room would observe a minute of silent prayer "for the souls of those departed members who have left us since last we met."

As the somber, silent minute gained weight, grew ponderous and all but unsustainable, the Unc's best tobacco field accents crackled over the loudspeakers from the microphone next to him on the table.

"Now that you mention it," Henry drawled, "I ain't feelin' any too good myself."

For an eternal second the room was stunned, and then the laughter exploded. Henry had done it again, and I loved him for it. At seventy-nine, he was still a southern boy in the big city.

Well, now that you mention it, I ain't feelin' any too good either.

About ending this book, I mean.

Writing about fishing is the best way I know to make a living. Because you have to do the fishing first. When you write about it, you get to do it over again. To my knowledge, no one has come up with a better way to enjoy life.

And I've got a lot to look forward to. In a week or so, Jeffrey will take delivery of his brand new Maverick and her brand new Evinrude. Now that the tarpon are here and he's become such a well known flats-fishing guide, he's about booked up through June. But a year ago, I reserved three days in May, and we'll go back to the Marquesas. Who knows, this year I may not screw up.

And John Graves will be on his way soon. I'll be able to tell him I've abided by his counsel and become a fly fish-

215

erman through and through. We'll go fishing together in his homemade flats boat and, who knows, between the two of us, we might jump a tarpon or two. I practice my casting almost every evening in the small park across the street from our house, and Jeffrey is teaching me to tie a Bimini twist, an Albright, a Rhodes loop, and the other knots I need to know. Soon, I may even start tying my own flies. When you're a fly fisherman, there is no end to the mysteries waiting to be solved.

I should have a surprise for John when he arrives. A construction crew doing some demolition work on a small island across the bay from where I work here in Key West left a flat-bottomed aluminum boat behind when they finished the job. There is just enough room on the deck of its scow's bow to stand and cast a fly rod and, with its outboard pulled up, the old john boat draws less than eight inches: just right for the flats.

Tomorrow, I'm hauling it to the shop. I'll build a wooden deck over its bare bones metal bottom, enclose the open transom, put in a seat or two, some rod racks, and brackets to hold the pole I'm going to make. And, in what may be my best plan yet, I'm taking a cue from my days with Wyman Aldrich and adding some quiet oarlocks and a pair of long oars. If I stand up and row, looking toward the bow, as I used to row my dory, I can put Jean or John right on top of a school of tarpon. With me at those silent oars, we won't need any electric motors.

Now that's something to look forward to, isn't it?